How to Become the Firm of Choice

Win the Best Clients, Recruit the Best People, Increase Profitability

ROBERT J. LEES AND AUGUST J. AQUILA

Dedication

Bruce W. Marcus (1925–2014)
A pioneer in the field of professional services marketing,
friend and mentor

Jack Gabarro
Friend, colleague, and mentor, without whom this book
could never have been written

Head of events and books
Leah Darbyshire

Commissioning editor
Laura Slater

Editorial assistant
Edward Bowes

Published by
Globe Law and Business Ltd
3 Mylor Close
Horsell
Woking
Surrey GU21 4DD
United Kingdom
Tel: +44 20 3745 4770
www.globelawandbusiness.com

ISBN: 978-1-78358-272-3
A catalogue record for this book is available from the British Library

Contents

Part 2

Introduction

When David Maister published his seminal book, *Managing the Professional Service Firm*, in 1993, professional service firm markets were relatively unsophisticated, with little competition for either clients or people.

In the intervening years to 2007 when Rob and his co-authors Tom DeLong and Jack Gabarro published their best-selling book, *When Professionals Have to Lead*, professional service firm markets had become much more competitive. The global players in the accounting and legal markets had drawn away from the pack, leaving the other firms feeling the cold winds of true competition for the first time.

But today's markets make 2007 look benign. Competition is fierce across all segments of the market and with increased regulatory scrutiny also impacting firms' actions, only the sheer scale of the global firms protects them from some of the buffeting faced by other firms. Now, we are seeing competition driving some firms out of business and an ever-increasing number of firms merging in the belief that with size comes safety. But, it does not. Even the global players, as Arthur Andersen would testify, are not immune from the ravages of competition.

Safety, and the opportunity to grow and progress, only comes from clarity around which services should be sold into which industry sectors, to which clients, and critically how they should be delivered, and by whom. With all of those decisions being relative to competitors. No firm competes in a vacuum and if firms are going to win in today's markets, decisions about how and when to compete necessitate a strategy based on not just their own but also their competitors' actions – even those they might not be aware of yet.

Probably the only thing we can predict with any certainty is that competition will only get tougher. So, how do firms break out of the pack and put themselves in a position to enjoy sustained success?

Our answer is simple: firms have to make an explicit decision to become "the firm of choice" in their chosen markets. And, in doing so, they must move their operations to the next level. So, what do we mean by the next level?

So, what is the next level?

Every firm operates at a specific level. What it does, and how it does it, generates its revenue and, ultimately, its profit. Of course, firms can increase profit by adding profitable service lines to their offering or by reducing their labor costs, to name but two possible actions, but that is not what we mean by the next level.

Taking your firm to the next level means analyzing every aspect of the firm's operations and improving the way they are carried out. Nothing is sacrosanct.

Ensuring all of the firm's internal operations and processes are aligned with what the firm needs to do to be successful in its markets becomes one of the key drivers. Also, the firm must have an absolute commitment to being the best. The next level brings with it a refusal to accept the status quo alongside a belief that the firm can always do better.

And doing better is always relative. Being the firm of choice means always being better than your competitors. Making sure that you are the firm that targets the right industries and clients, recruits the people who will make a discernible difference to the firm and its clients, and develops them faster and more effectively than other firms.

In our thinking, becoming the firm of choice and continually striving to move to the next level are absolutely intertwined. Being the firm that people and companies want to come to isn't a one-off. With competition getting ever tougher, firms must focus on sustaining that position – a challenge which forces firms to continually reassess their position and to strive to be even better.

An invitation to a firm's retreat

Dear Reader,

We would like to invite you to join the partners of Samson, Boyd & Johnson (SBJ), a mid-size law firm in the New England area, as they wrestle with how to take their firm to the next level – to become the firm of choice in their chosen markets. You may decide to be an observer watching the events and decisions of the partners as they unfold or you can become an active participant by adding your suggestions and proposals from your knowledge of your own firm.

Whichever you decide, you will find this book is written as more of a story than as a traditional business book. Our aim is to tell the story in a way that helps our readers understand the challenges of becoming the firm of choice and, critically, how to do it. As such, it contains a weath of practical lessons and advice.

You will be absolutely familiar with the challenges our firm faces. They are the challenges all firms have tried, or are currently trying, to address, but which few firms have come close to resolving completely.

Part One sets the scene. The opening chapter sees Cliff Johnson, the firm's current managing partner, musing over the major challenges the firm is facing and closes with his belief that, if the firm is to survive, it simply cannot continue to do what it is doing now.

The subsequent chapters in Part One include Nathan Taylor's description of what his firm, Kaufmann & Vales, did to move to the next level (*Nathan's story*). This is followed by Mark D'Angelo (an external consultant) walking the partners through how the retreat will work. He suggests the partners should have in their minds a model of what the very best firms do as they think about what SBJ should do in the future (*Mark's opening comments*).

In the following chapters, the partners are split into five teams (Markets, Clients, People, Financial, and Underpinning Beliefs) to address the issues Cliff and Mark have identified. Each team is asked to come up with the key issues they believe need to be dealt with. The chapter *What we agreed to agree* summarizes the teams' conclusions.

Part One concludes with closing comments from both Cliff and Mark. In his comments, Mark reinforces, through the use of a new model of professional service firms in action, the inter-relationship of the activities in professional service firms and the need for the teams to work together in coming up with solutions to the issues they are investigating (*Mark's closing comments*).

Cliff's closing comments signal the end of the retreat, with the partners scheduled to meet again two weeks later.

After opening comments from Cliff and Mark, Part Two moves straight into each team's findings and proposals. The teams have grasped the importance of working closely on their proposed solutions – just as they have understood that they don't have to have all of the answers and should look to other professional firms for best practice. The Markets Team, for example, uses the Practice Segmentation in Professional Services matrix that Mark had been taught, and the People Team uses an article on best practice in learning in their proposals for upskilling the firm's people.

When all of the teams have discussed their proposals, Mark leads two sessions on *Making it happen*. In the second of these, *Change is tough*, Mark walks the team through his accumulated knowledge of how to ensure any change initiative in a professional service firm is successful.

Cliff briefly takes center stage again when asked by Mark to respond to the question, *What do we do with the partners who don't want to join us?* Mark then reprises his model of professional service firms in action (*A picture is worth a thousand words*) before handing over to Cliff for him to close the retreat.

By the time we get to Part Three, *Two years later*, Cliff has retired and Kate Wellington has replaced him as managing partner. And the wheel has gone full circle as Kate is describing what SBJ did to move to the next level to another firm in her international association trying to do the same thing. Kate's talk details the results of SBJ's change initiative – how they became the firm of choice in their chosen markets, their financial results, what worked and what didn't, and what they could have done better.

Finally, Part Four provides all the exhibits and key concepts presented in the book.

We hope you find this book useful and a real addition to your critical thinking and strategic actions – and that it inspires you to help take your firm to the next level.

Rob Lees, London, UK
August Aquila, Minnetonka, MN

Cast of characters

Cliff Johnson, managing partner of Samson, Boyd & Johnson (SBJ)
Cliff is the second managing partner in the 60-year-old New England firm of Samson, Boyd & Johnson. Cliff started with the firm right out of university and quickly progressed. At age 28, he was the youngest associate to be named partner. William Boyd, the firm's first managing partner, took Cliff under his wing and while Cliff learned a lot from William Boyd, he also developed his own style over the years. The partners trusted Cliff to always do the right thing and he never let them down. Cliff recently became a grandfather and is looking forward to spending more time with his grandson.

Nathan Taylor, managing partner of Kaufmann & Vales (KV)
Nathan, MP of Kaufmann & Vales, passed the bar 24 years ago and worked for Kaufmann, Jones & Nagel until their merger with Vales & Partners four years ago. Nathan is originally from Concord, Massachusetts and moved to California to go to law school. He now lives in San Francisco with his wife, Pattie, and their two sons, Nathan Jr. and Jack. He has never given up his allegiance to the Boston Red Sox.

Mark D'Angelo, outside consultant
Mark has extensive experience working with the leaders of professional service firms in both the US and abroad. He has worked with the largest of the international accounting and law firms, as well as many small and mid-size firms. His services range from strategic planning to organizational design, human resources, and change management. Prior to becoming a consultant 15 years ago, Mark worked for one of the Big Four accounting firms as their Chief Learning Officer. A keen runner, Mark tries to do a couple of marathons every year but has to admit that his times are getting slower! Mark lives in Chicago, Illinois, and has three daughters, Shelly, Jen, and Terri. All of them are Cubs fans.

Kate Wellington, potential successor to Cliff Johnson

Kate Wellington has been with Samson, Boyd & Johnson for 20 years, starting with the firm right after college. An international tax specialist, Kate has been on the firm's management committee for six years and has been an integral part of helping the firm grow and stay on course. Recently, she has become Cliff Johnson's right-hand person and has led many of the firm's most important projects. Kate has two children, a son, Cary, who is attending a state university, and a daughter, Grace, still in high school.

Acknowledgements

No book is ever written without the help of countless people who challenge writers to dive a little further into the topic, write with more clarity, and question the relevance of their topics. We want to acknowledge and thank the following individuals who assisted us in this book. Without them we know that the book would be lacking.

Firstly, we'd like to thank the real Nathan Taylor. "Nathan" asked that his firm's case study be disguised and that he wasn't identified. However, although disguised, Nathan's story describes what happened as the real Kaufmann & Vales struggled to up its game and move to the next level.

But Nathan wasn't the only contributor to our thinking, and we'd also like to thank:

Greg Barber, President, Schenck SC; Wayne Berson, CEO, BDO USA LLP; Bob Bunting, Principal, RL Bunting Consulting, and former Chief Executive Officer, Moss Adams; Rick Francis, Partner, Abdo Eick & Meyers LLP; Nigel Haddon, Managing Director, Haddon Consult; Patrick J. McKenna, internationally recognized advisor to the leaders of premier law firms; Mike Mister, Partner, Møller Professional Service Firms Group; and Nick Page, Chairman, Bond Dickinson LLP.

And, finally, we would also like to thank Emily, Kate, and Daphne, who supported us through this journey.

About the authors

Robert J. Lees is the co-author, with Harvard Business School professors Tom DeLong and Jack Gabarro, of the best-selling *When Professionals Have to Lead: A New Model for High Performance*. He is also co-author of the HBR article "Why mentoring matters in a hypercompetitive world". Rob also co-authored, with August Aquila, *Engaging Partners in the Firm's Future* and *What Successful Managing Partners Do.* He has also published numerous articles on professional service firm strategy in both the US and UK.

Before retiring last year after 25 years working with leading professional firms across the world, Rob had spent the last ten years consulting with firm leaders on how to improve their strategic position and, critically, how to deliver it. During this time, Rob also helped set up Møller Professional Service Firms Group, the UK's leading PSF consulting firm.

Rob held several notable positions prior to moving into consulting, including global head of human resources at EY and head of EY's global leadership institute in Cambridge, Massachusetts. He was also head of professional development in EY's UK firm and director of professional development at Morgan Stanley.

Rob currently collaborates on selected research projects and writes on issues relating to firm strategy and performance. He can be reached at roblees2@sky.com

August J. Aquila is an internationally known speaker, consultant, and author and has held leading positions in the accounting profession for more than 30 years. He held several executive leadership positions with American Express Tax and Business Services, Inc., was a partner in a top-50 accounting firm in Chicago, and regional marketing director for Coopers & Lybrand in Chicago.

August specializes in helping firms develop performance-based compensation plans, transitioning firms from one generation to another, creating transformational strategic plans, conducting dedicated M&A searches, and taking firms to the next level.

In 2004, 2007, and 2009 to 2015 he was selected as one of the "Top 100 Most Influential People in The Accounting Profession" by *Accounting Today*.

He is the author of hundreds of articles and several books on practice management, mergers and acquisitions, and compensation plan designs. Recent books include *Engaging Partners in the Firm's Future* (Bay Street Publishing), *What Successful Managing Partners Do* (Bay Street Publishing), *Performance is Everything* (AICPA, 2012), *Compensation as a Strategic Asset* (AICPA, 2007), and *Client at the Core* (John Wiley & Sons, 2004).

He can be reached at aaquila@aquilaadvisors.com or 1-952-930-1295. For more information, see www.aquilaadvisors.com.

Part 1

Where to begin

Samson, Boyd & Johnson LLP, is a 60-year-old New England law firm that has grown from its two founding partners, Benjamin Samson and William Boyd, to 21 partners today. Samson and Boyd had worked together for six years at another firm before they decided to start out on their own. They came from a firm with a culture that fostered an "eat what you kill" environment. They left so that they could create a firm that would put clients first, was more collegial, and had fewer political distractions and issues.

From its humble beginnings in a one-room office, the firm has grown to three full-service offices in its region and employs more than 100 professionals and 60 support staff. The firm became outstanding at serving clients and the two founders were very well known and respected in the business community. Both Benjamin and William were loved by everyone in the firm. William was always seen as the conscience of the firm, making sure that it always did the right thing. During its early years, nothing ever went out of the firm to a client that did not cross William's desk.

SBJ is, in many ways, like so many other professional service firms today. It's successful, the partners are making a good living, and few partners leave, other than to retire. With the key leadership positions being held from appointment through to retirement, the firm's leadership has rarely changed. All of which made William's retirement and the addition of Cliff Johnson's name to the firm's masthead when he became the new managing partner a major change. In fact, not seeing William Boyd in the managing partner's office was probably the biggest change the firm had ever experienced.

When Cliff took over, he kept the firm profitable during some initial rocky economic times. Ultimately, the economy turned around and the demand for the firm's services increased. And, for many years, the firm did not have to do much differently to grow because business just walked in the door.

Now it was Cliff's turn to pass the leadership baton. Times had once again changed and history seemed to be repeating itself. The economy was again weak and the demand for services was no longer as strong as it used to be. Cliff wondered if the next generation of partners had the determination to do what he had done. Would they pull together and do what was necessary? The one thing Cliff was sure of was that the firm couldn't just stay the same. Things were different now and, in some ways, he was glad he wasn't going to have to deal with today's markets and client expectations.

While Cliff still had a voice in the firm, he decided to call a series of partner meetings to discuss the realities facing the partners as he saw them:

- How are the current markets having an impact on revenue and profitability?
- Can the partners reach a decision about what they ultimately want to do?
- Are the current group of partners fit to become the future leaders of the firm?
- How and where should they start diagnosing the issues?
- What specific actions would the firm have to take to become the firm of choice in its chosen markets?
- Becoming the firm of choice in its chosen markets meant upping the firm's game. So, what did they need to do to move to "the next level"?
- When they arrived at the next level, how would they measure success?

These and many other questions were raging through Cliff's mind as he tried to get ready for the first meeting. He knew he could not lead his partners to the next level by himself. So, in order to make the meetings and the change process more successful, Cliff invited Nathan Taylor, the managing partner from a very successful law firm in California, to talk to the partners about what his firm had done to up their game. Cliff also asked Mark D'Angelo, who had helped Nathan in his firm's journey, to facilitate the meeting. Cliff felt he needed to set the stage properly if he was going to make any progress as, ultimately, it would be up to his partners to do the heavy lifting.

He knew that the partners in any professional service firm are a hard team to convince. They think that if they are experts in one field that makes them experts in all fields. So, Cliff was determined to help them understand that wasn't true!

Cliff asked Nathan to describe the good, the bad, and the ugly of what Kaufmann & Vales did to get their partners focused on the task in hand.

Oh no! Not another bloody meeting!

The partners of Samson, Boyd & Johnson were just like partners of most professional services firms – they hated meetings and hated change even more. Once the partners heard about the upcoming meeting, they started to build their fortifications.

The older partners just wanted a quiet life and to keep looking after their clients. Many of them were close to retirement and they didn't want their dreams of sitting on a sunny deck with a glass of wine, or spending more time with their grandchildren, disturbed by having to deal with "all of this change stuff".

Many of the younger partners weren't sure what to do. They had grown up in tough environments but they had never faced one as tough as this before. They were a little hesitant and even a little scared.

The partners in the middle thought something needed to be done but, whatever it was, they preferred to leave it to "management".

The challenge facing all of them was how to ensure they had something urgent to do on the day of the meeting!

Cliff's opening remarks

The day of the first meeting finally came and Cliff was more than a little nervous.

"Good morning folks. It's great to see you all here. No one had an unexpected client meeting – amazing! But seriously, I'm really pleased you're all here as this is a really important time for the firm.

"As you know, I'm retiring shortly and whoever the baton passes to needs all of your help if the firm is going to prosper in these turbulent markets. We all know times are exceptionally tough and I think it's more than safe to say that this may be the new normal. If that's the case, the one thing I'm sure of is that we can't continue the way we are. In my 18 years as managing partner, the firm has faced some difficult challenges but we've always seen them out – admittedly, with some pain at times, but we've always come back stronger. And stronger is what we'll need to be again.

"A lot of our competitors have grown from strength to strength. In addition, over the last few years some smaller firms have grown to become a major irritant. We also have seen an increasing number of larger national and super regional firms entering our territory and trying to take our clients. So, if we are to succeed in the future, we need to be absolutely clear who we are competing against. And that means being absolutely certain which markets we want to compete in, who we want as clients, and which services our clients need and can afford to buy. Right now, we tend to be all things to all people. I know it's not actually as bad as that, but we're not as focused as we need to be. So, my challenge to you all is to find that focus and make our firm the firm of choice in the markets we want to compete in.

"We clearly have a number of big questions to answer and I want us to start the ball rolling today. We need to think big, to not accept our current reality or be defeatist. We have all the knowledge and ability in this room that is needed to drive the firm forward. In my view, there's no firm with our ability; we just need to harness our collective strengths and move the firm to the next level. This means we all have to work together, put our individual differences behind us, and think of the firm first. And, of course, of the firm's people. Remember, we are responsible for the livelihoods of the hundred and forty people who work for us. If we fail, we fail them and that's not part of any reality I see as acceptable.

"I know you are all up for the challenge, so let's get started. I know you've all heard of Kaufmann & Vales. Indeed, a lot of us have worked with their partners on different deals over the last few years. But, I doubt that many of you know that they also had to face up to changing markets and client needs. I've known Nathan Taylor, Kaufmann & Vales' current managing partner, for nearly ten years and have followed his career with interest. But what really heightened my interest is what Nathan was doing about four years ago when I began to notice a change in Kaufmann & Vales' strategy. And it's that change in strategy that I've asked Nathan to talk to you about this morning. The similarities between Kaufmann & Vales and our firm are remarkable so please listen carefully to what Nathan and his firm did. There are definite lessons here for us."

Nathan's story

"Good morning. My name is Nathan Taylor. Cliff has asked me to talk to you about what we did at Kaufmann & Vales to improve our firm's performance. Before I do that, a little bit of history to set the scene. Kaufmann & Vales was created four years ago following the merger of Kaufmann, Jones & Nagel (KJN) and Vales & Partners. At the time of the merger, both firms had offices in the same three cities and nine equity partners. KJN had revenue of $7.5 million compared to Vales' $6.5 million, and both firms' profits per equity partner (PEP) were within $10,000.

"From a financial perspective, it was a compatible merger but figures don't tell the whole story. The two firms had been 'dating' for several years and had come close to merging before, only for KJN to pull out when it became clear that Vales & Partners wasn't willing to sort out their underperforming partners and address their overdraft problem. Eventually, though, Vales & Partners sorted out its debt and partner issues and, with some of the older partners from both firms opting to retire, the new firm started with eleven equity partners, operating out of five offices across the state. Most of the partners were in their early to mid-forties and none of us had ever managed anything other than a small practice area."

No job description

"To my particular surprise, given my leadership experience was limited to running KJN's small litigation practice, I was asked to become managing partner. Despite some misgivings, including my preference for doing client work, I accepted. Naturally, the first thing I did was to look for the MP's job description, only to find that there wasn't one! So, with what was effectively a free hand, I set out on a path that I hoped would demonstrate that I could live up to the trust that had been placed in me. I found the first few weeks really scary and, at times, I was clearly out of my depth. Like all of my colleagues on the journey, I was a very capable technical lawyer who had a good rapport with his clients but, unfortunately, none of us was close to being either a rainmaker or a leader.

"But, I had to start somewhere, and so I did – by analyzing the firm's performance data. And that revealed a worrying trend. Our markets were extremely tough and, like a lot of our competitors, our revenue and profitability were relatively flat. What was more worrying was that some of our best clients were giving work to our competitors that they had previously given to us. Definitely, not a good place to be.

"We had to do something to ensure we retained our clients, as well as win some more. I set about trying to decide what we needed to do. Conscious that everyone was waiting for me to do something to justify my new title and salary, I instituted several different initiatives – some of which worked and some of which didn't. As I fiddled, so to speak, our markets got tougher and the firm needed more than my relatively inexperienced tinkering.

"Facing up to my own lack of expertise wasn't easy, but, like lots of managing partners from firms around the world, I opted to take myself to a top business school to learn what I didn't know. I had a really great week at the program and, when I came back, I was all fired up and even more determined to change the way the firm did things. 'Alignment' was my new buzzword and I quoted its virtues to everyone!"

Three strategic options

"At the first partners' meeting, soon after I got back, I presented three strategic options I had devised on the flight back. The first was more of the same – the firm continuing to concentrate on both personal and commercial law. The second was to increase our commercial law practice from around 30 percent of revenue to at least 50 percent. At that time, we didn't really know precisely what work was available. It was more of a belief that commercial rather than individual was where the future lay. The third was to build the firm to a position where it was a target for acquisition by a larger, probably regional, law firm.

"The debate was pretty straightforward. None of the partners wanted to work for someone else so option three was out immediately, and option one was deemed unrealistic given the way the markets were moving. So, option two was something of a 'no brainer'. We needed something to aspire to (our vision, if you like) so we decided that we wanted to be the 'local' alternative to the regional/national law firms – or 'big law' as we called them.

"It was obvious that life as a partner was going to have to be different in this new world, so we identified the key areas of a partner's activities and developed key competencies and key performance indicators (KPIs) for each of the areas.

"We focused on the basics. If we could get this right, we would be successful:

- Winning business;
- Developing people;
- Leading and managing the firm;
- Improving technical knowledge; and
- Managing matters with efficiency and profitability.

"We all signed up to the changes and, while we wanted to make progress in each of the areas, we all decided that we needed to concentrate on improving our capability in winning business, especially from our existing clients."

Change is not linear

"Ideally, I'd love to walk you through the initiatives in the same topic-based way, but change doesn't happen in a straight line. The reality is that what you do in one area nearly always impacts another, so change has to be seen as holistic – a series of interrelated initiatives, which, over time, lead to changes in the way the firm does things and, ultimately, to an improvement in economic performance. Consequently, I'm going to take more of a time-based approach and, hopefully, that will match our learning experiences step-by-step and make the story more realistic.

"As we thought about winning more business, we realized that there were other critical things we had to deal with.

"In a lot of ways our journey might never have got off the ground at this point as I was faced with a groundswell of opinion, which, put simply, said 'but we're already good at this'. Despite knowing that we all weren't, saying so was pointless, so I decided to get our top clients' perspective by asking them what they thought.

"In every case, our clients really liked their partner and the fact that we were local. But in every case they also said that they only knew that single partner in our firm, whereas they had been introduced to lots of other partners in our competitors' firms.

"There's no doubt that the feedback from our top clients was the clincher that taught me an important lesson. In order to convince your fellow partners to change, you need to win the intellectual argument before you can win the emotional one. You need real data not just opinion!"

New business development

"Our first decision was to recruit a business development director – one who had experience working in 'big law'. We found our candidate, Tom Bergman, quite quickly. Tom rapidly set about improving our profile in our markets. He also introduced activity-based KPIs, like the number of network events attended, in order to stimulate some activity, and he started working directly with some of the practice areas and client teams.

"All of which made perfect sense and we were all extremely pleased with the rapid increase in our profile that actually going out into the market yielded. However, uneven activity across the partner team caused some partners to complain and feel slighted. There were increasing accusations of 'Tom was just talking a good game and was not interested in helping some of the teams'. These accusations were obviously damaging, especially as all of the activities hadn't actually generated any significant increases in revenue. I suppose, on reflection, we didn't do our due diligence well enough. The focus on activities, which seemed smart at the time, was never the right approach. So, after 20 months, we let Tom go. We had had a lot of activity, but weren't very much further ahead."

Our next attempt

"Despite that, or in some ways because of it, I still had a mandate to get some new business development support so we went into the market again – this time, thankfully, successfully! Without doubt, Amy Cisneros was a real find. She was much more supportive of the partners, providing them with coaching and helping them figure out how to uncover their clients' needs and win more business. And, when they needed additional support, Amy actually went out with them to see clients. It was Amy's coaching approach that persuaded some of the partners that they could step outside of their comfort zones and take the occasional risk. She also scrapped the simple activity-based KPIs!

"So, at last, we were starting to make progress on the business development side, but sadly not on the other aspects of how we needed the partners to think and what they needed to do. I just wasn't getting any real traction and all of my best efforts to persuade my colleagues to think about the firm, rather than their own or their practice's revenue, were falling on deaf ears. And it wasn't for lack of trying. I wish I could say it was, but I had put a lot of personal energy into trying to get my colleagues to take on more of a leadership role in both the firm and its people. Although they agreed that they needed to do it, they continued to do exactly what they had been doing before. I felt I was failing, and not even the Red Sox could lift my spirits!

"I really needed help to inject some urgency into our efforts, but didn't know how and where I should get it. The answer was simpler than I thought. I asked the MP of another firm, who had also been on the business school program I attended a couple of years earlier, what he did. He pointed me toward Mark D'Angelo. After several enjoyable and fruitful discussions, I asked Mark to help us."

Getting traction

"We called another partner meeting. We walked the partners through some of the ideas and concepts I had learned from the business school program in the hope of generating similar enthusiasm. Some partners took the ideas on board. Others, though, were more than happy to say, 'that's Nathan's responsibility' when anything remotely managerial or leadership related came up.

"The truth of the matter is you don't gain sufficient traction until all of the partners are going in the same direction. So I started to have some difficult conversations with the underperforming partners and with those who clearly did not share the firm's values and vision. I also encouraged other partners to play a part in persuading their colleagues to go along, as peer pressure often has the greatest impact

"We had, also inevitably, brought in some new partners with expertise in B2B work. We were building a strong cadre of talented partners. But we also focused on developing the expertise of our associates, bringing in a rigorous coaching program, and ensuring the associates attended technical and practice events.

"While all of this sounds great, and it was a big step forward, I felt that we weren't moving fast enough. We needed much more urgency if we were going to make it through the extremely tough times we were facing."

Our "road to Damascus" moment

"And then our big break happened. It was an absolutely unplanned result. But we found out that that's the way some things happen when you undertake a change initiative. You embrace it and use it and move on at speed!

"The big break was putting our 40 lawyers through a training program on value pricing. The outcome went way beyond pricing philosophy. All of a sudden, our lawyers realized that they didn't have to give discounts before they had even entered the room, and that price was a negotiation. Believe me, it was a 'road to Damascus' moment! They all got their self-belief and self-confidence back. Instead of being the butt of their clients' demands, they began to see themselves as equals again. A major and welcome change! That was our first break.

"The second break was a result of our business development/sales training. Along with the pricing program, this program gave our people the skills and confidence they had lost and dramatically improved morale. Partners actually went out expecting to be successful. And they were, as we saw a 12 percent increase in revenue almost overnight!"

Professional services is an execution game

"Despite our success in winning more business, we never lost our focus on our people. Every time I spoke to Mark, he reminded me that professional services is an execution game and that increasing your people's capability faster and more effectively than your competitors is a competitive advantage. To make sure we continued to focus on our people, we ramped up our training and introduced a mentoring program. Everyone in the firm was given free choice in choosing a mentor and the only restrictions we put on it was that you had to choose someone outside of your current team. No one was allowed to have more than two mentees. At first, we were concerned that free choice was a risk, but it wasn't. Everyone acted truly responsibly and endeavored to do the best for themselves, their colleagues, and the firm.

"Well, that's our story and I hope you found it interesting and helpful. We are very proud of what we have achieved and, just to illustrate how far we have come, our revenue has increased 60 percent since the merger and our PEP even more. We still operate out of the same five offices, but we now have 25 partners and are the firm to work for in each of the cities. Oh, and our client feedback is exceptional!

"But, before you ask whether we're happy with where we are, the answer's 'no'. There is always a next level. We still have issues with some of the partners failing to step fully up to their leadership and managerial responsibilities. I come from the school that believes that the partners are the leaders in a professional service firm. What they do sets the tone for what everyone else does and how the firm responds to its many constituencies. So, yes, there's still work to do in this area. No matter how successful we feel we are, we can never afford to rest on our laurels. We have some great competitors out there and we know they'll never rest on theirs."

Questions from partners

One partner asked, "With the benefit of hindsight, what did you feel you did not do?"

Nathan reflected, "There are actually two things I wish I had done sooner. The first is that I didn't push hard enough. Being the managing partner of a smaller firm can be difficult. You typically know everyone really well – and sometimes their families, too. So, you're often pushing people you call friends. And the reality is that I didn't push the recalcitrant ones hard enough.

"The second was not involving the non-partners earlier in our process. If I had, I might have been able to generate some upward momentum from the associates to complement my downward efforts and force faster change. But it's a learning process and you continue to learn as you progress on the journey. I am sure you will find that out as well.

"Finally, I learned that the role of a managing partner is similar to managing a portfolio of different businesses. Not all practice areas operate in the same fashion or are in the same place. With the firm's vision in mind, each practice area needs to determine what the next level looks like for them, what they want to do, and how to get there. The managing partner is there to help them reach the next level by providing guidance and support, and by ensuring they work together and come up with actions that take the critical interrelationships that exist in a professional service firm into account.

"Well, if that's all of the questions, I'd like to thank you for your attention. I hope I wasn't too long or boring. Enjoy the rest of your meeting!"

Rules

Cliff was extremely happy with Nathan's remarks and saw that the kick-off went well as many of his partners were nodding their heads in agreement with Nathan. Now was the time to get Mark involved!

"Hi everyone, my name is Mark D'Angelo. As you know, I met with each of you individually over the last few weeks to find out what you thought were the challenges facing the firm and I'll be running through these very shortly.

"But, before we get started, I just want to outline a few rules that will make the day more productive for all of us:

- Let's begin with the end in mind. We are here to make a good firm even better by identifying specific goals and responsibilities.
- We need everyone to participate. This is your responsibility.
- Success will only come about if we work together and deal with the issues as a team, rather than as a collection of individuals pushing our own viewpoints.
- There is no hierarchy today. Everyone is equal.
- No topic is off the table.
- If you have something to say, please share it with the entire team. We don't want any side conversations or comments.
- It's critical that we attack the issues and not the person. Be honest with yourself and others. Differences of opinion are healthy, but please, if you don't agree, share your reasons.
- Refrain from telling war stories. All of your partners have heard them many times already.
- Be positive, focus on how to get things done.

- Share your ideas – there is no such thing as a dumb idea, at least for today!
- You have to trust what your fellow partners decide. If you don't, you need to explain your reasons.
- Finally, please make sure you turn off your cell phones!

"That's it, so let's begin."

Mark's opening comments

"Let me share with you what successful firms have in common when it comes to addressing change. I don't think that anyone would ever question that a firm's success is ultimately tied to its partners' performance and behavior. And yet, getting partners to work together is one of the key issues facing the majority of firms and their leaders today.

"So, before you can work on change, we need to work on getting you involved and committed to the firm's future. I know from experience that you won't be committed to the future if you haven't had any involvement in deciding what it should be. And if you aren't committed, then you essentially work for yourself and not the firm.

"You are the culture of the firm – what you believe, what you reward, what you do, and how you do it determines what gets done, and how things get done. And, if you don't believe in what the firm is doing, you will never be effective role models who think 'firm first' and actively bring the whole of the firm's services to your clients. Ultimately, it's going to be up to you to make things happen. You are the drivers of the initiatives. It will be up to each one of you to make the firm successful and make it the firm of choice.

"I want to follow a basic three-step process with you today. First, we are all going to work on identifying the issues facing the firm. Second, we are going to split into five teams. Each team will discuss one of our issues. I am going to ask you to select a team that you want to be in. This should be a topic that you are passionate about and that you feel you can add a lot of good content to. Third, I'll ask each team to provide serious proposals or potential solutions to the issues. Each team's thought process will be shared with the entire team half-way through the day and again at the end of the day.

"But, before we start, there's a question we need to think about first and that's, 'change to what?' Cliff talked about our being the firm of choice in our chosen markets and that's a great aspiration. So, if we assume that the firms who are 'top of mind' right now are there because they do things in a particular way, the questions for us are:

- What do they do?
- How do they do it?
- How can we incorporate their practices into what we do?

"To answer the 'what do they do' question, I'd like to share with you some research by two colleagues of mine, Rob Lees and August Aquila, on what the best firms do. There are a lot of best practice studies out there and you may have read some, but the problem with most of them is that the firms are pre-selected and it's only their practices that are studied. Rob and August took a different tack, believing that there are lots of great practices in lots of firms and that pre-selecting a small number of firms means you never find out about them So, their approach was much broader. Their research takes best practices from the over 250 firms with whom they've consulted across the world, from their colleagues like me, and from extensive desk research. And these are their findings."

Mark put the following slides up and talked briefly through each of the best practices:

What successful firms do

They have a clear vision and strategies for getting there

- There is a shared understanding of what to do and shared commitment to its achievement
- They make tough choices, always focusing on continuous renewal
- The partners role model the behavior needed to deliver sustained success

They think markets as well as clients

- The partners continually scan the competitive environment
- They anticipate market changes and look for opportunities to enhance their service offering
- Having decided what to do, they invest in the resources needed to deliver

They develop a deep, deep client orientation

- Their reputation for delivering outstanding solutions precedes them
- Companies actively seek them out
- They are part of their clients' "institutional memory" – the first port of call when the client needs help

The firm's people are as important as the firm's clients

- The firm is committed to helping its people develop their expertise either inside or outside of the firm
- "It's a hard place to be hired into, a hard place to be promoted, and a hard place to stay" – but, when people move on, they do so as friends
- The firm cares about its people, going out of its way to help with both work and personal situations

They have a high performance ethos

- Everyone in the firm positively wants to be the best
- People will go the extra mile
- People actively seek new solutions which force competitors to react

They are outstanding at execution

- They leverage ideas and expertise, regardless of their origin, to deliver client value
- People are confident enough to set stretch goals and push hard
- They focus on client solutions that are at the forefront of thinking

They embrace the "one firm" concept

- Loyalty abounds in the firm
- They downplay stars. It's the team not the individual that really matters
- There is an embedded set of principles and practices which maximize the trust and loyalty people feel for both the firm and their colleagues

They have a strong culture and shared values

- The firm has a culture of high challenge and high support
- Partners "walk together"
- People are intolerant of the "wrong" behavior

They have a highly collaborative style

- People go out of their way to help each other
- The focus is on team not individual
- People have confidence in their colleagues and proudly introduce them to their clients

They have strong partnerships

- Partners see themselves as custodians of the firm's future, creating an even better firm for the people who follow them
- Partners share and police the firm's vision, values, and strategies
- There is a premium on collegiality and discipline

They have an absolute commitment to recruiting the right people

- Top partners lead the recruitment efforts
- Cultural fit is as important as technical competence
- They downplay qualifications, focusing on the individual, not the piece of paper

They believe that developing their professionals is at the core of the firm's beliefs and activities

- Partners pass on their knowledge and expertise – continually and actively
- Coaching and mentoring are part of the foundation of the firm
- The focus is on "growing your own" rather than bringing in lateral hires

They are committed to staying at the top

- People always look for new ways of doing business
- They continually draw input from multiple and diverse sources
- Coming second isn't acceptable

Mark could see some of the partners beginning to look daunted by the list. He didn't want to lose them, so he said:

"Look, let's be realistic. I don't know any firm that does all of these things perfectly. It's about continually moving forward. Think of each of the above points as a continuum. For example, if I draw a line and place weak partnerships at the far left and strong partnerships at the far right, there are countless positions between the two where a firm can find itself. As a firm moves to the right, the partnership becomes stronger:

"And, if we look at another continuum, the same thing applies:

"As I just said, no firm does all these things perfectly, although some firms clearly do some things much better than others. The smart thing is to assess where you are in relation to what the best firms do and then figure out how you can improve what you do. Sometimes that may mean doing things a lot differently; sometimes, it may mean hardly any change at all.

"The key is for us to be honest about where we are now and to put together very specific plans that will get us to the next level as quickly as possible. Getting things done quickly and well is really important. Having great plans is one thing, turning them into reality is another. We all know that some of this may be tough, but the upside is being the firm of choice – and that's absolutely worth fighting for.

"So, let's get to work!"

Mark's findings

Mark reminded the partners what Nathan had said earlier in the day:

> *"No matter how successful we feel we are, we can never afford to rest on our laurels. We have some great competitors out there and we know they'll never rest on theirs."*

Mark knew that all firms have to evolve with changing market and client demands. Staying still isn't an option. This was clearly brought home in Samson, Boyd & Johnson's case when Mark reviewed their recent history and completed his one-to-one interviews with the partners. This is what he found and shared with the partners that morning:

- Revenue had been flat for the last three years
- Net profit remained flat in the last four years
- Two up-and-coming associates had left the firm for opportunities at competitor firms
- The firm lacked a clear direction
- Some partners were disengaged from the firm. They were more worried about themselves and focused on building their silos
- Markets had become really tough, yet the firm continued to do the same old thing
- Competition was fiercer than ever
- Clients were awarding work to different firms
- Competitors were adding new services
- The best candidates were not joining the firm
- The firm had to address the succession issue

In reality, all of the partners already knew these challenges existed, but didn't know what to do, or worse were afraid, to address the issues. It was up to Mark to stimulate the discussion and get the challenges on the table. Just preaching about the dangers of these issues would not be sufficient. Mark had to convince each partner to tackle the issues. Only when each partner was committed to do something differently, could the firm move to the next level.

Categorizing the issues

Mark listed the issues on the white board without any personal comment. He then asked the partners to think through these issues and to add any more they thought were relevant. To help the categorization process, Mark identified the five main drivers of professional service firm performance: markets, clients, people, financial, and underpinning beliefs.

Using a white board, he captured their additional thoughts under the five headings:

Markets

- Markets are really tough
- Competition is coming from many new competitors
- Competitors are offering new services
- Competitors are cutting prices
- We are serving each market segment the same way we always have

Clients

- Clients are spreading work among different professional service firms
- Clients are becoming more sophisticated
- Client needs and expectations are changing
- Revenue from core service lines is decreasing
- Clients are more demanding
- Clients are more price sensitive
- Clients want more value for their fees
- We are not winning enough business

People

- Best recruits are not joining the firm
- Firm is losing its up-and-coming associates
- Loss of experienced people will create succession issues
- Partners are becoming disengaged
- Partners are grumbling about issues rather than addressing them
- Associates are complaining that their friends get better training at other firms

Financial

- Revenue has been flat for three years
- Revenue from core service lines is declining
- Net profit has remained flat for three years
- Gross margins are down
- WIP days outstanding are increasing
- Clients are slower to pay
- Firm is not firing unprofitable clients

Underpinning beliefs

- Firm seems to be drifting
- No clear direction
- We accept things as they are, not what they should be
- There seems to be no urgency/things happen to us, we don't take charge
- Our compensation is not aligned with strategic issues
- We lack a clear performance management system
- Our partners don't lead

Let's get to work!

"Alright", Mark said. "It time for each of you to select one of the five main drivers of professional service firm performance (markets, clients, people, financial, and underpinning beliefs) to tackle as a team. I'd like you to choose a driver based on your interest and knowledge so that you can add value to the team.

"First, I want each group to develop a list of questions that will help the firm to address the issues that need to be answered. Keep in mind that these issues are interrelated and when we change one it has an impact on the rest of them.

"I want you to prioritize and identify the top three-to-five questions in each area, and then present them to the whole partner team at the end of the session. Remember, nothing is off the table, even if you suggest that the firm has too many partners!"

The partners broke into work teams and started brainstorming questions to consider. No question was too dumb or unimportant during this stage of the process. Finally, each team selected a spokesperson to provide feedback at the end of their work session.

The work teams had two hours to come up with their questions before reporting back to the entire team. Mark quietly monitored the teams to make sure they were staying on track. At the end of the two hours, he called the five teams together and started the debrief.

"Alright everyone, it's time to see what questions we need to answer. There are two steps in this process. First, each team will present all of their questions and then, second, explain why you selected the ones you did for future analysis."

Markets questions

Marvin, one of the firm's litigation partners, presented the Markets Team's questions. As he was speaking, Mark captured the team's thoughts on the white board. These are the questions the team came up with:

Markets Team questions

- Do we have a brand that is recognizable?
- Is there brand consistency?
- How loyal are our clients?
- Do we really know where our revenue comes from?
- Do we deliver services in the most efficient and profitable manner?
- Do we know how our services segment and how important each one is?
- Are we offering the right services?
- What services are our competitors offering?
- How are our services viewed compared with our competition?
- Do we know what to do to succeed in each segment?

"As you can see", Marvin said, "we came up with a fairly long list of questions to consider. We struggled with many of them and had some very good discussions. Our problem, initially, was that we were confused about what we meant by market. In the end, with some help from Mark, we settled on the market for services because that's what we sell. And, alongside that, what we need to do to ensure we deliver the different types of services we offer in different ways.

"But, at the end of the day, we knew we had to pare down the list to a more manageable number of questions. So, here are the three key questions we need to answer:

Markets Team key questions

- Do we know how the market for services is segmented and how profitable each segment is?
- What do we need to do to be successful in each of our segments?
- Do we know what services our competitors are offering and how they deliver them?

"The Markets Team selected these questions because we felt the firm didn't know which segments we were competing in and the importance of each segment. Each practice team basically delivers its services in the same way. So, they use the same utilization and leverage targets regardless of what service is being delivered. This seemed okay yesterday, but not today!

"As well as delivering every service as if there were no difference between them, the team clearly recognized that we didn't really know what drove success in any one segment, other than delivering our real estate services to small and medium-sized clients. And, probably worse, we have no real idea what our competitors are doing now, or are likely to do in the future. Data, we now believe, is fundamental to the firm's success.

"Our partners probably have much of the data the team needs, but no one has ever seen the value of capturing it before. In closing, the Markets Team needs your help. Rack your brains and send us anything that might help us get a picture of what is going on competitively – no matter how small or seemingly insignificant."

Clients questions

The Clients Team came up with 17 questions during their brainstorming session. Jennifer, a third year partner, led the discussion. She first outlined all of the questions the team considered and Mark captured them on the white board:

Clients Team questions

- Who are our core clients?
- What do they want from us?
- How do we want them to perceive us?
- What do they buy from us and from our competitors?
- What do they value?
- What do we know about them and their business?
- Do we know which industries are growing or shrinking?
- What data about our clients do we have?
- Why have we lost clients?
- Why don't we win more proposals/opportunities?
- What's our reputation in the market?
- What do our clients think about us?
- What do our clients think about our competitors?
- Do we know who the most profitable clients are?
- What types of services are our clients no longer using?
- Which clients make us money?
- How do we want our clients to perceive us?

Jennifer then began to explain what her team had discussed:

"I'm sure that each team had some heated discussions. I know we did. The Clients Team first addressed this question: 'What do clients really want'? Well, the question was easier than the answer. In general, this is what we believe all clients want.

"Clients have issues and problems that they are grappling with. That's why they seek out professional advice. They want a professional who has the skills and experience they need to solve their problem or help them to seize an opportunity. We also know that clients have a wide choice of professionals, and they know there are options.

"Clients today are also more sophisticated and they no longer blindly accept the advice of the professional without questioning, challenging, or demanding more reasoning and detail! And, because of the complexity of business today, clients demand that their professionals know more about their business and industry.

"There is also the question of trust. Clients will only trust us if they know we care about them and their business Yes, we have to know about their business and what's going on in their industry, but it's more than that. It's about providing insights that demonstrate that we understand who they are and what drives them. Creating that personal trust is what earns us the right to influence clients.

"With these thoughts in mind, we selected five questions where we wanted to get additional information. So, here are our key questions:

Clients Team key questions

- What do our clients buy from us, and what do they buy from our competitors?
- Which clients make us money?
- How do clients perceive us?
- What do we know about them, their business, and their industries?
- Why have we lost clients?

"We had universal agreement that we couldn't answer these questions on the spot and we would have to do some research. Some of our partners clearly have more knowledge than others to help us answer these questions. So, if you know anything, please talk to us."

People questions

ɔw the People Team's turn to present their questions. This team p with a long list of questions that needed answers. This made since it is the people in a professional service firm that really make ifference. Mei Zhen, a relatively new partner who was known to be d with people, took the lead in the discussion.

'Our team identified 17 questions. I know that's quite a lot, but there ere so many things we didn't know. It also became abundantly clear to ɔur team that we couldn't answer some of these questions until we had answers from the other teams like, which markets, which services, and what our clients expect.

"Here's our list:

People Team questions

- Do we have the right people in the right roles?
- Can we attract the talent we want?
- Do we reward the right behavior and capabilities?
- Do we have effective training programs?
- Do our learning and development initiatives deliver the capabilities we need?
- Do we keep the people we want?
- Do we advance people at the right time and speed?
- Why do people leave us?
- What are we really good at?
- Are the partners and managers good coaches?
- Do our teams work as well as they should?
- Do we have the right bench strength?
- Do our people ask for help?

Financial questions

It was now the Financial Team's turn. The partners were beginning to see how the various pieces were fitting together. Mark reminded them of what Nathan had said earlier in the day.

> *"The reality is that what you do in one area nearly always impacts another, so change has to be seen as holistic – a series of inter-related initiatives which, over time, lead to a change in the way the firm does things and to an improvement in economic performance."*

Gail, who was the firm's finance partner, spoke for the Financial Team. They realized that without making changes in the previous three areas, there would be little likelihood of success in the financial arena. The only way the firm was going to improve its financial performance was through better training and direction for the people delivering services to the clients who wanted them – and who were willing to pay for them.

Gail listed the questions, emphasizing particularly the need for the client analysis as it would help answer one of the Client Team's questions about which clients make the firm money – and, of course, which don't.

Financial Team questions

- What is our range of net realized rate per hour by client, by type of work?
- What should be our acceptable gross margin on our clients?
- How do we increase utilization by level?
- How do we improve realization?
- Can we increase partner/staff leverage?
- How do we justify higher rates?

- What is an acceptable level of net income per partner?
- How do we manage and contain cost?
- What should we be doing to make investments for the future?
- What do people spend their non-billable time doing?
- Do we have the right processes to achieve our financial goals?

She then continued:

"Everyone here knows that numbers are near and dear to my heart. But I also realize that we have to get behind the numbers and find out what is driving them. Just saying that we want a 10 percent increase in profits next year is not enough. We need to decide how to achieve it and then do it. I'm excited about the path we are going down and am convinced, more than ever, that we need to get our areas aligned in order to move up to the next level. The Financial Team's top three questions are:

Financial Team key questions

- What is our range of net realized rate per hour by client, by type of work?
- What should be our acceptable gross margin on our clients?
- What should we be doing to make investments in our future?

"You are probably wondering why we selected these three questions and not others. Well, we need to know what is our most profitable work, and who are the most profitable clients. When client X calls screaming for help and client Y calls at the same time, whom do we give preference to?

"We will always take some work that is not as profitable as we would like. We do a lot of non-profit work in the summer months and the margins are less than desirable. That's okay as long as we agree as a team to do it. What we don't want to do is take on more work during busy season that does not meet our desired profitability levels.

"Finally, we need to be making some investments for the future. There is a cost for doing this, but we need to explore new markets, services, systems, and so on that will build capacity for us down the road. We are no different than any other business. We need to make money today in order to stay in business tomorrow, but we also need to work, so to speak, on research and development that will build capacity in the future."

Underpinning beliefs questions

The last team was ready to make its presentation. The partners had put in a lot of work during the day and they could now see the challenges ahead of them.

Annette, one of the firm's senior partners with more than 25 years of experience, walked the partners through her team's questions:

Underpinning Beliefs Team questions

- Do we have a common culture? If not, what are the differences?
- Do different practices/offices have different cultures?
- Do we actually go the extra mile for our clients, or do we just talk about it?
- Are we committed to each other?
- Are we adaptable? Do we find new ways to do things?
- Do we reinvent ourselves?
- Do we care about each other?
- Does everyone play a part in the firm's future?
- Does everyone care about the firm?
- Are we creating a "one firm" firm?
- How do we get the partners to walk together?
- Does everyone know what the firm is trying to achieve?
- Is everyone committed to doing outstanding work all of the time?

"We had a robust discussion when it came to selecting the top three-to-five questions. We kept asking ourselves 'why these?' All of them seemed important, and are. In the end, we felt that the following were key ones we needed to address first. If we could get these right, we would be on our way."

Annette handed out the team's five top questions:

Underpinning Beliefs Team key questions

- How do we get the partners to walk together?
- How do we make sure that everyone knows what the firm is trying to achieve?
- How adaptable are we? Do we find new ways to do things?
- Do we actually go the extra mile for our clients, or do we just talk about it?
- Do we have a common culture? If not, what are the differences?

"We want everyone in the firm lined up behind the firm's vision and we need to ensure that we, the partners, are at the forefront of that vision. We have to be seen as one, not fragmented; otherwise, how will we be able to convince any of our people that we all want the firm to succeed? It's basic stuff, really. Just as it is that we go the extra mile for our clients and that when we have to change, we do so quickly. In fact, we must anticipate changes not just react to them."

"And, of course, there's the question of a common culture, where we all subscribe to the beliefs that drive the firm and should drive what we do. We all know that's not the reality right now. So, our team wants to know what's stopping people, and especially us, from doing that. This shouldn't be a tough task. We all care passionately about the firm; it's our livelihood, our profession, and our life. We have to make sure we create a firm that will continue to prosper for us and for the people who follow us. After all, that's what being a partner is all about."

What we agreed to agree

Everyone had to agree that these were indeed the top questions for each category. If anyone entertained reservations, Mark asked them to explain their doubts. Another robust discussion ensued.

Finally, the partners agreed to suspend any disagreement or concerns they had for the greater good of the firm.

Yes, they had agreed to agree!

Top markets questions

- Do we know how the market for services is segmented, and how profitable each segment is?
- What do we need to do to be successful in each of our segments?
- Do we know what services our competitors are offering and how they deliver them?

Top client questions

- What do our clients buy from us, and what do they buy from our competitors?
- Which clients make us money?
- How do clients perceive us?
- What do we know about them, their business, and their industries?
- Why have we lost clients?

Top people questions

- How do we know we have the right people in the right roles?
- How do we gain an understanding of the capabilities we need to be successful, and where our real capabilities lie?
- How can we attract the talent we want?

- Do our learning and development initiatives deliver the capabilities we need?
- Do our people consistently strive to be better? If not, why not?
- Do we reward the right behavior and capabilities?

Top financial questions

- What is our range of net realized rate per hour by client, by type of work?
- What should be our acceptable gross margin on our clients?
- What should we be doing to make investments in our future?

Top underpinning beliefs questions

- How do we get the partners to walk together?
- How do we make sure that everyone knows what the firm is trying to achieve?
- How adaptable are we? Do we find new ways to do things?
- Do we actually go the extra mile for our clients, or do we just talk about it?
- Do we have a common culture? If not, what are the differences?

Mark's closing comments

Mark congratulated the partners on their work during the day. The partners planned to meet in two weeks and Mark wanted them to come back with specific answers to the questions, and with distinct proposals to move the firm forward.

"Let me remind each of you that you cannot work in isolation. You need to check-in with each other, to talk to your colleagues about what you are doing and what they are doing, and to think holistically about the solutions you come up with. You have to ensure there are no suggestions that impede your momentum because they are miles apart. That's not to say there has to be complete agreement with every detail. That would be unusual at this step in the process, but ideas and suggestions ought to be going in the same direction. If they aren't, and one team remains convinced they're right, bring them to the next meeting and we'll debate them together."

Before he let the team go, Mark went back to his earlier comments about the interrelated nature of the activities in professional service firms.

"Earlier, Nathan and I spoke about the interrelated nature of activities in a professional service firm, but few models actually illustrate this interconnection well. I've been working on a model with some colleagues which we believe does that well and I'd like to share it with you before you go.

"Okay, let me walk you through the model, which we call the Professional Service Firm System and Beliefs Model©. A mouthful, I know, but here we go."

Mark kept the slide up so that he could refer to it, and also to keep the partners focused on it. He began by telling them that all businesses, including professional service firms, are dynamic systems in which one element has an impact on another, and that the model identifies the key elements and illustrates the non-linear nature of their interaction. Mark could see some of their eyes clouding over and knew he had to get more practical.

Professional Service Firm Systems and Beliefs Model©

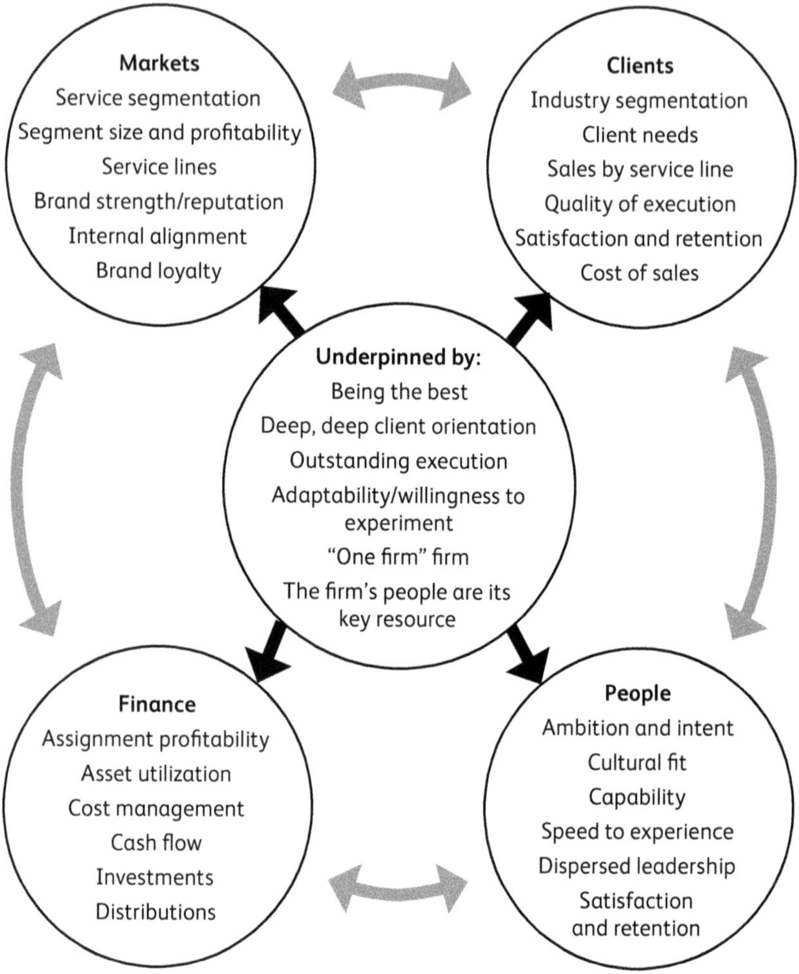

"Okay", he said. "I want to illustrate the model in action and it is easier to view the interactions between the elements as if they were linear. You can start anywhere in the model but, for the purposes of this example, let's start with Brand strength/reputation in the Markets circle."

"Brand strength/reputation is the result of delivering outstanding services to the right clients in the right markets. It's one of the key drivers in attracting top people and top companies as clients. When you're a top

Professional Service Firm Systems and Beliefs Model in Action©

firm in the market, people with the capabilities, ambition, and the intent needed to keep pushing the firm forward, will want to join your firm since good people always want to be associated with a winning firm.

"Additionally, when these people are the beneficiaries of outstanding learning experiences and the type of encouragement that comes from dispersed leadership, this enables them to do more interesting work quicker (what we call 'speed to experience'), their level of satisfaction goes up – as does their desire to stay with the firm. This commitment to the firm and its client also brings with it a commitment to go the extra mile and constant efforts to find better ways of doing things.

"The alignment of these experiences and behaviors with a commitment to the firm's ethos of being the best and its deep, deep client orientation delivers substantive increases in the quality of execution – which, in turn, brings with it increases in client satisfaction and retention, which, of course, increases brand loyalty and brand strength.

"With increased brand loyalty and brand strength comes additional work from existing clients and new work from new clients, both of which bring increases in utilization and profitability. When clients use additional services, the additional work typically lowers the cost of sales.

"More work provides more opportunities for people to progress, which, in turn, further increases their level of satisfaction with life in the firm – with the resultant positive impacts on service quality and client satisfaction.

"These continued positives drive further increases in profitability and investment. And the cycle starts over. The top people want to join you, execution quality goes up, top companies seek you out, profitability increases, and brand strength grows ever greater.

"One final thing, nearly every firm talks about putting its clients first, but not every firm succeeds in delivering the quality of execution that ultimately leads to the level of brand strength and loyalty which drives competitive advantage. Brand strength occurs only if firms recruit the right people and provide them with a high level of learning experiences. This needs to be done within a 'one firm' culture which emphasizes the individual's importance to the firm and encourages its people to constantly do things better in the future.

"So, there you have it!"

Cliff's closing comments

"Thank you all. It's been a very long but productive day, a great start to our unleashing the potential we have and becoming the firm of choice in our chosen markets. I couldn't be happier, as I can see a bright future for us that is exciting, challenging, and profitable.

"I'd like to finish the day by echoing Mark's comments about working together, about remembering that all of us in this room have the firm's future in our hands. They're great hands and I'm looking forward to when we get together again in two weeks and decide how to create a firm that will deservedly dominate its markets and deliver a rewarding future for our people and clients."

Part 2

Two weeks later

The big day of sharing solutions had finally arrived. Cliff was excited to see what the teams had come up with. Over the last two weeks, he could see the teams coming together. Not wasting another moment, he let out a hearty "Good morning all!"

"It's great to see you all here and I know we're going to have a great day. Mark will be joining us again to facilitate the day's progress. We are going to apply the same rules as we did last time we met.

"So in case you forgot them, here they are:

- Let's begin with the end in mind. We are here to make a good firm even better by identifying specific goals and responsibilities.
- We need everyone to participate. This is your responsibility.
- Success will only come about if we work together and deal with the issues as a team rather than as a collection of individuals pushing our own viewpoints.
- There is no hierarchy today. Everyone is equal.
- If you have something to say, please share it with the entire team. We don't want any side conversations or comments.
- It's critical that we attack the issues and not the person. Be honest with yourself and others. Differences of opinion are healthy, but please, if you don't agree, share your reasons.
- Refrain from telling war stories. All of your partners have heard them many times already.
- Be positive, focus on how to get things done.
- Share your ideas – there is no such thing as a dumb idea, at least for today!
- You have to trust what your fellow partners decide. If you don't, you need to explain your reasons.
- Finally, please make sure you turn off your cell phones!!

“Remember, there is no hierarchy today; we’re all equal. So, it’s especially critical that we listen carefully to what each of us says. I’ve been listening to some of your conversations over the last two weeks, so I know that you have the firm’s best interests at the forefront of your thinking.

“I know from all of the conversations I’ve had with the teams, and some of you individually, that a lot’s been happening in the last two weeks. The Financial Team tells me they’ve been inundated with requests for data and they’ve done their best to help everyone. The Markets Team the same. But what’s been really amazing has been the buzz around the offices. I can’t remember the last time there was so much energy around and so many positive vibes. It’s just great! It makes me think I should reconsider retiring! No, just kidding!

“Thanks again for coming and let’s have a great day! Mark, over to you.”

Mark's opening comments

"Thanks, Cliff. I'm also really excited about today. I've been working with all of the teams over the last two weeks and I'm absolutely delighted at the commitment you've all shown and the way you took my words about the interrelationship between the firm's activities to heart. So, without further ado, let's get started.

"The plan for the day is that we'll go through each team's work in the following order: markets, clients, people, financial, and underpinning beliefs. Each team will take any questions for clarification at the time, but I'd like to park any substantive questions of content until all the teams have finished presenting. That way, we'll have a more holistic picture before diving into any specific questions and their consequences.

"After we've dealt with any questions and agreed to the five sets of content, we'll spend the rest of the day developing our plan, putting the puzzle together using the model I showed you at the end of the last meeting. But that's for later. For now, let's listen to Marvin's Markets Team present their findings and proposals."

Findings and proposals

Markets Team

"To refresh your memory, I'm showing the list of questions and proposals that the Markets Team prepared for today's meeting on the screen."

Markets Team questions

- Do we know the markets for services segments, and how profitable each segment is?
- What do we need to do to be successful in each of our segments?
- Do we know what services our competitors are offering, and how they deliver them?

Markets Team proposals

- Prepare an in-depth analysis of our services segments
- Analyze how we go to market
- Determine what success looks like in each segment and compare that to how we go to market
- In conjunction with the Clients Team, analyze each segment to find out which industries and clients our firm serves, and to what scale
- Have the firm's marketing department conduct a competitor analysis

"Alright everyone", Marvin shouted over the various conversations. "We all know that understanding our markets is critical, and our team has made a start. I have to admit, we struggled initially but Mark shared with us a way of understanding how the market for professional services is segmented that he'd studied when he attended a class taught by Harvard's Jack Gabarro. This gave us the kick-start we needed. The matrix is on the screen now and, while I'm not going to run through every aspect of it, you'll see how it works when I run through our conclusions with you.

Practice segmentation in professional services

Standardized	Customized	Expertise-Driven	Rocket Science
Client Problem: Efficient solutions to common problems	**Client Problem:** A tailored, but still relatively low cost, solution to a common problem; guidance through the pre- and post-purchasing process	**Client Problem:** A major complex and ill-defined issue that the client has little or no experience of	**Client Problem:** A major "bet your company" issue that the client has no similar experience of
Key Skill: Efficient, low cost delivery of established methodologies, models, and processes	**Key Skill:** Providing user-friendly advice which generates confidence in the selection process and thereafter	**Key Skill:** Real-time diagnosis and judgment	**Key Skill:** Providing innovative and novel solutions
Critical Success Factors: Established methodologies, models, and processes; efficient and low cost delivery systems	**Critical Success Factors:** Established methodologies, models, and processes; efficient, low cost delivery systems; inter-personal/relationship skills; managing the "sales" costs	**Critical Success Factors:** Experience of similar problems; in-depth technical and/or functional knowledge; exceptional relationship skills	**Critical Success Factors:** Highest level diagnostic skills; creativity; state of the art knowledge; pioneering concepts
Profit Drivers: High volume, high leverage	**Profit Drivers:** Above average fees; good leverage	**Profit Drivers:** High fees; low leverage	**Profit Drivers:** Premium fees; very low leverage; may also refer work to others
Selling Proposition: "Better, faster, cheaper"	**Selling Proposition:** "Use us, we'll tailor the solution to you and your needs, and provide you with ongoing support"	**Selling Proposition:** "Trust us, we've seen similar problems before and we'll help you over your problems"	**Selling Proposition:** "Smartest brains around"

Adapted from the original matrix, ©Rob Lees and Jack Gabarro, which is included in When Professionals Have to Lead, *Harvard Business School Press, 2007*

"There are some obvious realities as you move from left to right across the matrix. For example, if you are operating in the Standardized Segment, you will be competing with multiple providers and there will be little differentiation. The opposite is true if you are in the Rocket Science Segment, where there are few competitors and differentiation, compared to other segments, is high. And, as you can imagine, the Standardized Segment yields relatively low margins, which necessitates high volumes to generate adequate levels of profitability. The critical thing that Mark kept reminding us of, though, is that you can make money anywhere along the matrix; it's just about tailoring the offer and the delivery to the market.

"When we compared our services to the matrix, we found that most of our services are in the first column, the Standardized Segment. However, some of our high-end tax consulting and M&A advice is in the Expertise-Driven segment. We discovered two problems, though. The first is that we deliver our services in exactly the same way no matter which segment they are in. The second, as you'll hear more about when Jen runs through what the Clients Team has done, is that we don't do enough to personalize our services to move our clients across the matrix into the Customized Segment. And, as a result, we don't maximize our profitability. This has become a real eye-opener for our team.

"Our discussions about going to market made us realize that we always go to market the same way, no matter what the service. This was definitely our old way of doing business, but we are currently looking at how we can reconfigure the delivery processes. For example, whenever we have to deliver standardized services, we need to look at our staffing model and make sure we don't overstaff or use more senior staff than we need. We're still working this through but hope to have finished the initial analysis in two weeks. It may take a few days longer as we need to do some random sampling of different types and sizes of jobs and work with the Financial Team to establish margins.

"As far as the competitor analysis is concerned, we're well on track. I want to thank you all for the valuable information you provided. It's amazing just how much we know about other firms. It's even more amazing that we've never collected it before! Anyway, I expect the marketing department will have completed the report in a couple of weeks. But, please, don't stop sending in any information that you get. In fact, may I suggest that if you've got anything you think should be shared, just do it! Send an email to us all, copied to marketing, and that way we'll all be in the loop.

"Okay, that's it from our team! Jen, over to you."

Clients Team

Jennifer reminded the partners of the Clients Team's five key questions as she put the following slide up:

Clients Team key questions

- What do our clients buy from us and what do they buy from our competitors?
- Which clients make us money?
- How do the clients perceive us?
- What do we know about them, their business, and their industries?
- Why have we lost clients?

"As you can see, a lot of our work dovetails into the work that the Markets Team is doing. Together I'm confident that we will get a much better understanding of our clients and how we should be going to market.

"The next slide covers the six proposals that we think are critical to help move us to the next level. I'm sure that some of them are a bit controversial since we have never ventured down this path before. So, if there are any questions about them, now is the time to ask."

Clients Team proposals

- Prepare an in-depth market analysis of our clients and their industries
- Conduct interviews with our top 20–40 clients to determine what work we are not getting
- Work with the Financial Team to analyze the gross margins we get on our top clients
- Work with Markets Team to develop a questionnaire to understand client perception of the firm and satisfaction
- Provide industry research and training for partners and managers to help them understand our clients' businesses
- Interview lost clients to determine why they left us

"Alright everyone", Jennifer shouted. "I knew some of these proposals would get some attention, but I can't answer everybody's questions at once.

"As Marvin has just said, we need to be much clearer about which services make us money. We have been working very closely with the Markets Team, combining our research to make sure we have actionable conclusions.

"We know we can't be all things to all people, and not knowing what services our clients need (both now and in the future) can lead to wasted effort, time, and money. So, to make sure we do know where to focus our efforts in the future, we are also working with the marketing department to get a better understanding of the industries our clients operate in so we can better predict future needs. But we are also trying to predict which markets will grow and which will decrease over time. And, of course, if there are likely to be any new markets we haven't thought of yet! That's a distinct possibility given the speed technology is changing right now!

"Originally, we had a much longer list of things to consider, but as we met and discussed the issues, it became clear that what we really needed was to understand our various markets and how important each one is to us now and in the future. We also realized that tackling the first three projects was key, and so we've concentrated our efforts on these.

"The first thing we tackled was the definition of a market so that we all agreed on what we were discussing. After some time, and with Mark's help, we decided on the following definition which you now see on the screen."

What is a market?

A market is a group of potential clients with a common need where we have the services/products that can satisfy the need.

"Obviously, whether it's a successful market for us depends on our ability to persuade potential clients that our offerings are better than those of our competitors. Let's remember that a market, after all, is not what we have to sell, but what people in the market want to buy."

Jennifer finished by asking the partners what questions they had, and if they wanted to discuss the first proposal further. After a couple of brief questions, Jennifer began to address the team's second proposal.

"In our second proposal we want to set up interviews with our top 20–40 clients to determine what work they are giving to our competitors. And why, of course."

One partner said, "You actually want us to talk to our clients about these issues? I'm not sure they'll tell us, and why should they?"

Jennifer answered, "I'll share our experience with you in just a moment."

She knew that her team's proposals were going to scare some of the partners, but she also knew that the only way to get accurate information was to go to the source. She did not want to get into a confrontation at this stage though. Jennifer's experience before coming to Samson, Boyd & Johnson confirmed that clients appreciate being asked for their input. If the firm was ever going to meet their clients' needs, she knew that the partners would have to get closer to the clients by knowing them better.

Jennifer continued with her presentation.

"Do you remember what Nathan, the managing partner from Kaufmann & Vales, said at our first meeting?

> *'There's no doubt that the feedback from our top clients was the clincher and it taught me an important lesson: when you're dealing with professionals you need to win the intellectual argument before you can win the emotional one. You need real data not just opinion!'*

"We've already taken this message to heart by interviewing two of our top clients! First, we worked with the marketing department to develop a list of questions we wanted to ask, and David and I each talked to one of our top clients last week. Believe it or not, we enjoyed each meeting! Our clients were happy to see us and to answer our questions. That's not to say everything went smoothly. In fact, it didn't, but it was pretty consistent. In each of the interviews, our clients said how much they valued our technical expertise. In fact, they both said that they always came to us first when they had thorny technical problems. They knew we'd always have some constructive ideas.

"Sadly, we did less well when it came to our knowledge of the client's business and of being proactive with ideas. Our clients both said that while they know lots of our competitors' partners, they hardly know any of ours. Obviously, we're poor at introducing and recommending our colleagues to clients, valuing their expertise, and expressing our confidence in them and their work – and it's costing us.

"David's client, which is one of the firm's premier clients, also said that they thought we weren't always abreast of industry trends and so they are thinking of using one of our competitors to do more of their work.

"So, if we go back to the practice segmentation matrix, you can see how very important it is for us to be able to tailor our solutions to each client's needs. When we do that, we'll not only be able to increase our fees, but also to provide a higher level of service.

"The clients were really pleased that we came to them and clearly wanted to help us succeed. If the rest of our top 20 clients are the same, we have a great opportunity to get much closer to our clients and their opinions. And, that can only be good! We'll also have some great data on which to move forward.

"As far as our third proposal is concerned, the Financial Team has already started the analysis of gross margins on our top 20 clients and they are due to let us have the results in the next few weeks. We are looking forward to their report. While some of us may think we probably already know what the answer will be, we will have to wait to see if we are right or wrong.

"We'll be able to start thinking about the industry research and the relevant people training when the Markets Team has finished their analysis and we've put our heads together to look at which industries, which clients, and which services to focus on. I've already asked the HR team to think about how we can improve our ability to analyze market trends and our clients' businesses. I did try to persuade Cliff to let us all go to Harvard for the professional services program, but he wasn't too keen on that idea!

"So, all in all, we're pleased with what we've done so far. We've still got to sort out which companies and clients to talk to about business that we didn't get, but I think we've got a good start and more than enough on our plate right now!"

People Team

Mei Zhen represented the People Team once more. She knew she had some particularly important ideas and proposals to get across, a lot of them far from what the firm was doing now.

"Like the previous two groups, we've been very busy. We hope our proposals will resonate with you. While working with the Markets and Clients Teams we became aware that the linkages between their proposals and ours are particularly strong. Some of the things we're suggesting are a long way from what the firm does now, but if we don't address them with an open mind, we won't be successful. Change is not a judgment on the past actions of the firm. We must always honor the past and respect the future. We have been successful, thanks to many of the people in the room today. As a younger partner, I want that success to continue. So, let me share with you what our team came up with.

"You may recall the five key questions we determined at our first meeting.

People Team questions

- Where do our real capabilities lie?
- Are the right people in the right roles?
- Do our people constantly strive to be better? If not, why not?
- Are we rewarding the right behaviors and capabilities?
- What capabilities do we need to deliver through our learning and development initiatives?

"Like the other teams, we came up with a list of proposals to address these questions. I don't know if we've put too much on our plate, but we know we've got to tackle all of them. We are going to have to prioritize the tasks. For now, though, let me talk through the proposals that are on the next slide.

People Team proposals

- Analyze our non-technical and technical capabilities and compare them to market needs both now and in the future. Fill in any gaps in current and required capabilities
- Determine what standards are required to be the firm of choice and ensure that leaders drive performance to those standards
- Make sure that there is clarity about what people have to do. Help them understand what they need to do better
- Communicate the "new" firm to potential new entrants and ensure we recruit the people we want
- Develop a "world class" learning system

"First of all, let me say that we see a very different future, one that will have us working in a firm which will win the game. But to do that we need the right people doing the right things – delivering the outstanding execution that distinguishes the top firms no matter which profession we are talking about.

"Our team has taken the stance that, in order for the firm to attract the right people, we need clarity around which markets and which services we will participate in. So, we have focused all of our attention on ensuring our people know how to do the right things.

"And, I have to admit, we cheated a little! In our search to find out what other firms were doing, we came across a paper and some articles which provided 99 percent of the answers we were looking for. Not that we minded, you understand!

"So, with a little help, here we go.

"Let's start with our key proposal – create a 'best in class' learning system. This will enable our people to operate more effectively than our competitors. If you remember, in his model, Mark called this 'speed to experience'. The more we thought about it, the more obvious it was it's a clear competitive advantage. It enables our people to do more challenging work earlier in their careers, which then enhances our reputation with clients and prospects and, finally, will enable us to charge a higher rate for our services than our competitors.

"Not only do we need to consider everything (both technical and non-technical learning) an individual needs to know and do in order to operate effectively, we also need to remember that knowledge and experience are intimately linked. We have to make sure that whatever classroom learning our people get, they also get the on-the-job training they need to put it into practice with clients.

"I think it will probably be clearer if I show you a slide of the best practice learning model.

The best practice learning model

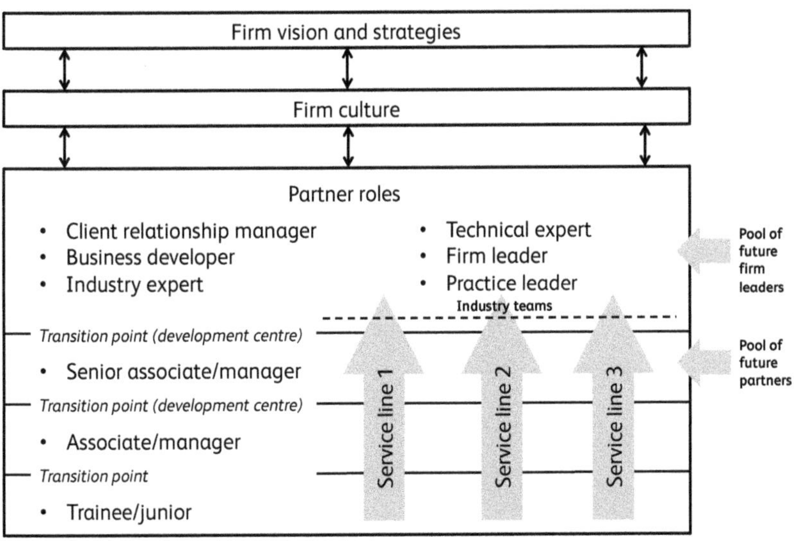

"In the best practice learning model, there are up to six roles that a partner can undertake. First, we need to define the roles and then identify the key capabilities for each of the roles. We have to do this at the partner level before we do anything else. Then, we can do it for each of the levels below partner. With these capabilities identified, we can then establish the core learning program for each role and level in the firm. Finally, we will have to make sure that everyone not only goes through the core learning, but is also able to apply what they learned in real-life client situations.

"Most learning is initially taught off-the-job. But it only becomes successfully applied when it is integrated into what people do. So, one of the key capabilities for all of our people is to be an effective coach. It is especially critical for partners, but all of our people have to be capable of providing constructive, actionable feedback which helps their colleagues to become even better at what they do.

"And, as you would expect, we also need to do a better job of taking individual development needs into account when we assign people to jobs. Another thing we need to get right is to help people through the different transition points, from staff to associate, associate to senior associate, and especially from senior associate to partner. Based on the concept 'forewarned is forearmed', we recommend programs designed to help our people understand the issues they will be facing and provide guidance on how to overcome them. This should help shorten the transitions and enable our people to be effective sooner.

"We had a lot of other thoughts about how to achieve the 'speed to experience' concept, for example:

- Development centers in which each professional's skills and knowledge are profiled against the capabilities required to operate at the next level. Then, an individual learning program is created to speed his or her development. I must say, this sounds like a great idea and I wish the firm had had this when I was coming through.
- Great mentors who can help you make your way through the firm are a huge asset. So, yes, we've all got to become much more effective mentors.
- Programs for high potentials are found in most of the best firms. We are very aware that this is an emotive issue in the firm, but we need to decide whether to have one or not. Our group is in favor, but it's obviously a decision for the partnership as a whole.

"If you have any questions or comments, now would be a good time to bring them up. We naturally have some thoughts on the content of the core learning programs but, other than saying that we foresee four streams of content – technical, winning business, analyzing businesses, and leading and managing teams – we think the details are best discussed after we've all agreed the way forward."

Four streams of content

- Technical – including project management/assignment efficiency
- Winning business – individually and in teams
- Analyzing businesses – understanding client strategies and positioning the firm's services
- Leading and managing teams – at assignment, practice, and firm level

"And, that's a good place for me to stop. Our group has unanimously bought in to the 'speed to experience' concept and the learning that goes with it. When we get it right, we have absolutely no doubt that we will have the ability to be the best firm in our chosen markets. It is Cliff's dream – and it's most certainly ours, too!"

Financial Team

Gail came to the meeting with the firm's financial and partner/associate production reports for the last five years. It was a good thing they were e-files and not actual paper files because she would have needed three more people to carry in all the documents! She came prepared with facts to answer any financial question thrown at her. That's what the other partners respected about her.

The first thing Gail did was to open her computer and project the team's first slide.

"Just in case you forgot, here are our team's key questions:

Financial Team key questions

- What is our range of net realized rate per hour by client, by type of work?
- What should be our acceptable gross margin on our clients?
- What should we be doing to make investments in our future?

"We realize that there are all sorts of statistics that we can look at. In fact, the team did consider a lot of them. For example, we looked at net fees per equity partner, billable hours for partners, realization and utilization rates. And while all of these are somewhat important in the grand scheme of things, we wanted to get beyond these basic statistics and ratios; otherwise, we weren't going to help the firm and the other teams get to the next level. In fact, our mantra was: what do we need to improve to get us to the next level?

"It's not just tracking the statistics, because they just become lagging measures. We want to be part of the change initiative in getting all of you to focus on the behaviors that will generate better financial results. So, with that introduction, let me share with you our proposals:

Financial Team proposals

- Analyze the firm's net realized rate per hour by client segment and by service segment
- Analyze the top ten clients by partner to determine average gross margins
- Determine what percentage of our profits should be allocated for investment projects that will build capacity for us in the future

"As you heard from Marvin and Jennifer, we are working with the Markets and Clients Teams to analyze the firm's net realized rate per hour by client segment and by service segment. We still have a lot to do, but I thought you'd be interested in the results so far. It's not going to be much of a surprise when I tell you that we don't have any work in the Rocket Science Segment. Nor that the clients in the Standardized Segment have the lowest realized rate per hour, or that the rates are higher in the Customized and Expertise-Driven Segments. The problem, as you heard earlier, is that the difference between the rates just isn't high enough. And with so much of our work, possibly as high as 80 percent, in the Standardized Segment, you can see why we have serious profitability issues.

"We embarked on this journey two weeks ago partly because of our flat profits and the great thing, as far as I'm concerned, is that we now have a starting handle on why and, much more importantly, what to do about it.

	Standardized	Customized	Expertise-driven	Rocket science
Realized rate per hour	$129	$157	$183	
Realization	73%	80%	84%	

"I can stand here and tell you to move your clients to the right to the more profitable segments, but just saying it won't make it happen. And that's why we need to take on board what the People Team is recommending and get all of our people, including all of us in this room, better skilled and more involved with our clients.

"We also did a quick analysis of our clients, and our analysis seems to back up 'Pareto's Principle'. Or, put another way, 80 percent of the profits come from 20 percent of the clients. This means that we are all going to have to make some tough decisions. There's no doubt that some clients will have to be fired and asked to find another firm. I've heard the term 'cutting the tail' used in some firms, and there's absolutely no doubt we'll be using it here.

"Obviously, decisions on what investments we want to make will come when all of our analysis is finished. We need to make wise investments in new markets, new services, people, and systems. We need to keep building our future capacity in order to grow and ultimately reach our vision of being the firm of choice.

"So, that's it. Short and swift, as they say, but you'll be hearing a lot more from us soon."

Underpinning Beliefs Team

Understanding a firm's history is central to understanding its current culture and values. And so the team chose Annette, who had a long history with the firm and the respect of the other partners, to speak for them. If anyone represented the values of the firm, it was certainly Annette.

She knew that every successful initiative in the past was the result of all the partners getting behind it, believing in it, and caring deeply about it.

"As you have heard me say so many times before, we need all of your support to be successful in this undertaking. I know we all have different goals in life. Some of us are looking forward to relaxing on a sunny beach with a glass of wine, while others are concentrating on funding their children's college education. But in order for each one of us to achieve our personal goals, we must be in agreement when it comes to our firm's vision and goals.

"Just like the teams that presented earlier today, our team decided upon key issues and proposals. Here are the key questions we all agreed upon at our first meeting.

Underpinning Beliefs Team key questions

- Do all the partners walk together?
- Does everyone know what the firm is trying to achieve?
- Are we adaptable? Do we find new ways to do things?
- Do we actually go the extra mile for our clients, or do we just talk about it?
- Do we have a common culture? If not, what are the differences?

"If we are truly going to become the firm of choice, then we need to make sure that our proposals become part of our firm's DNA; otherwise, we will just have some nice words on a sheet of paper.

"So", Annette continued, "how are we going to make sure that the answers to these questions are always 'yes' and that they are part of who we are? It's certainly not going to be easy. Our team is going to challenge you with some of the hardest and most critical activities we need to do in order to accomplish our goals. Here's our game plan."

Underpinning Beliefs Team proposals

- Create a "one firm" firm by reinforcing the partners' understanding of what it means to be a partner in our firm. And then help our partners create it!
- Communicate the firm's plan and initiatives to everyone in the firm using as many different types of media as possible. And keep doing it!
- Support the partners in driving a culture of innovation and change
- Look for great client service examples within the firm and publicize and promote them as best practices
- Identify, define, and provide examples of our shared values in action. Evaluate our people on how well they live the values and, when it's needed, help them live the values more consistently

"As you can see, that's a pretty comprehensive list of activities. We've already made a start on the first point and we'll have a straw man for us to debate next week. We plan to use teams of about six partners to debate the model, and then get all the partners together to agree upon the final document. After that, it'll be all systems go! We already know that one of the key things will be helping and coaching each other. We firmly believe we can only do all this successfully if we all do it together, and that should be what partnership signifies.

"Our plans for involving all of the people in the firm are simple. For the initial meetings, each office will get all of their people together to share our vision of becoming the firm of choice in our chosen markets. Then, the partners will ask our associates for their ideas on how we can improve what we do. We want to encourage all of our people to contribute and nothing should be off the table! It's all part of pushing responsibility down and having everyone contribute to creating the firm's future.

"We'll share, across the firm, what each office comes up with so we don't reinvent the wheel. That way, people will see that their ideas are being listened to and used. I know that in some offices and practices this is going to be tough, but we have to do it. Mark will be with us on this journey to help the offices facilitate the meetings. Our colleagues in HR will also be able to help us with the meetings.

"We'll include a discussion on values in this initial meeting as well. When every office has come up with their list of what they think our values should be, our team (yes, we want to stay involved!) will synthesize all of the output and feed it back to the offices for debate. It may take two or three iterations, but we're confident that, with this approach, we'll have a robust set of values that everyone will buy in to and support.

"We all know we have to do things differently, and our team is excited by what the firm can achieve. And we know that if we keep sharing the good stuff across the firm – the examples of how we've changed, the successful things we've done, the successes we hope to achieve, people will start to believe anything is possible. And we'll start to believe, too!

"Finally, we want to talk further with the firm's management team about tying some portion of a partner's compensation to living the firm's values and being a good citizen.

"If you have any questions, we can discuss them now. If you have ideas, additional information we can use, send it to me. We know we don't know everything. This is a journey for all us. But we are confident that with everyone's help we can develop a strong foundation that will sustain the firm going forward."

Making it happen

Because Mark had been through this process many times before, he knew that the hard work was just beginning. He wanted to plant the idea in the partners' minds that it would be up to them to make change happen. They would have to do the heavy lifting. And, while everyone felt good about doing that today, Mark knew they would have to change some of what they were doing now.

Mark brought up the next slide:

From...

- Undermining colleagues and the firm's initiatives
- Subverting ideas discussed at partner meetings
- Treating staff poorly
- Staying silent, not voicing objections when decisions are made
- Finding fault in everyone and every idea

To

- Supporting firm initiatives by participating
- Presenting evidence based on alternatives
- Treating all staff with respect
- Communicating concerns openly and providing alternative solutions
- Focusing on team members' strengths and helping them develop

"The only way that we are going to be successful in our new venture is if we all walk together. I want you to remember two things that Nathan shared with us about his firm's journey. First and I quote:

> *'I come from the school that believes that the partners are the leaders in a professional service firm; what they do sets the tone for what everyone else does and how the firm responds to its many constituencies.'*

'Second, let's remember that we can never rest on our laurels. We have some great competitors out there and we know they'll never rest on theirs.'

Mark waited a few minutes to let the partners think about these two important thoughts. It would be critical to keep reminding them of these and other key points in the coming weeks.

"To make sure we stay focused on the tasks ahead of us, I am asking each of the teams to follow a few simple rules.

"First, I want you to meet as often as possible, especially while we're in this critical phase, and to commit to having finished your work in no more than three weeks. This way, the teams can do all of the necessary integration so that we can debate all of the final analyses, proposals, and suggestions four weeks from today. Second, each team will provide subsequent updates to the entire partner team every four weeks. And, as we all now know, momentum is absolutely crucial! It will be up to each team member to keep his or her colleagues engaged and accountable.

"Finally, we are going to schedule the meetings now for the next 12 months. These meetings are as important, if not more important, than any client meetings. Once they are in your calendars, you must commit to them. Remember, we are now working on the most important client – your firm."

Change is tough

"Before we look at where and how to start putting your ideas into action, I thought it would be useful if I ran through the principles that relate to leading successful change in a professional service firm. These principles result from all my work, plus that of my colleagues, as well as extensive research and conversations with the leaders of professional firms across the world.

"So, here we go:

- **It's about the whole firm.** The firm comes first, second, and third!
- **The partners have to walk together.** You've heard this many times before!
- **Behavior only changes where the work gets done.** As partners, you have to ensure that your people take on board the new ways of doing things, of dealing with clients and each other, and don't fall back to the 'old' ways because it's easier.
- **You have to make the 'end' real; otherwise, it's only an abstraction.** We need to make sure everyone knows what and where the end is. It has to be definable. Everyone needs to know what success looks like.
- **Change isn't linear.** Remember what Nathan said at our first meeting. It would be great if it were, but some things just don't happen as planned.
- **Involve everyone in the firm as early as you can.** If you do this, they will feel ownership of the solutions and they'll deliver!
- **Over-communicate. Over-communicate. Over-communicate.** There is no such thing as over-communication during a change program. People get bored, get worried, get tired – you have to reduce their anxiety by keeping them informed of how far they have come, and how much they have achieved.

- **Encourage people to do things differently.** Don't criticize failure, or be afraid to fail. Rather, learn from it. And don't expect nor wait for perfection. Just because something doesn't work the first time doesn't mean that it is wrong, or that it won't work the next time.
- **Don't reinvent the wheel.** Bring people together to share what's worked and what hasn't. And spread the good stuff fast!
- **Take every opportunity that comes along.** Remember Nathan's story of the unexpected uplift in morale that came after the pricing and sales training programs. You never know what the future holds!
- **Instill a 'high challenge/high support' culture.** Lots of firms have the 'high challenge' but not the 'high support'. People should never be afraid to ask for help. Remember, it's about being the best. And people will make mistakes. The key is to help them, to learn from it, and to move on together.
- **Recognize people's contributions.** People want to be associated with success; it's uplifting and great for morale. Thanking someone can be more important than paying them more.
- **Know what you're good at – and what you're not.** When you need external help and support, get it. It'll speed the process and that's key. Use the unique strengths of everyone on your team.

"There are three key principles that are my favorites. So, don't forget them:

- **Make things fun.** Make the journey exciting. Make it worth the time, effort, and pain involved in getting there.
- **Although speed and momentum are critical, successful change typically takes time.** Ensure you don't get sidetracked by the classic spoiling tactic of 'add on', for example, 'When you're doing this, could you have a look at this… and this … and this… '

"And finally,

- **People will get 'change fatigue'.** Leaders have to be on the road, telling the story, emphasizing the reasons for the change and the benefits. All this work can be discouraging at times but, when the firm achieves its 'best in class' reputation, it will all have been worth it!

“I know that’s a long list and it probably appears very daunting – possibly even to the extent that you might be afraid to start. But it’s really not that bad. Just keep in mind that people usually want to go with you. It’s all about giving them clear direction, support, and help on the journey. If you do that, you’ll get there. And, you’ve got a brilliant, shiny end point. Who doesn’t want to be part of the firm of choice!

“Well, now it’s crunch time! We’ve heard some brilliant ideas and I’m sure you’re excited about the firm’s potential. I know I am. But now we come to the hard part – turning all of the ideas into reality.

“I’ve pulled two significant quotes from Nathan Taylor’s introduction. They are on the screen now:

> “It would be a lot easier if I could walk you through the initiatives in the same topic-based way, but change isn’t like that. The reality is that what you do in one area nearly always impacts another, so change has to be seen as holistic – a series of interrelated initiatives which, over time, lead to a change in the way the firm does things and to an improvement in economic performance.”

> “And then our big break happened. It was an absolutely unplanned result. But we found out that that’s the way some things happen when you undertake a change initiative. You embrace it and use it and move on at speed!”

“These two quotes sum up all of my experiences in dealing with major change. Quite simply, no change program I’ve ever known works as smoothly as people intend. Some things do, but some things just don’t. So, don’t become discouraged if something does not work out exactly as you expected. The key is to respond quickly to the new circumstances and put in place actions that take you back to where you want to be.

What do we do with the partners who don't want to join us?

One of the partners, who had said very little during the day, finally raised his hand and asked Mark, "What do we do with the partners who don't want to go on the journey?"

"You bring up a very important issue", said Mark, "but I'm not the person to answer it, Cliff is." On cue, Cliff got up and took over the reins.

"I know that not everyone is going to totally agree with everything we want to do. That's to be expected. We can understand and accept where they are coming from, but everyone has to be part of our journey. So, the deal has to be, we want everyone to be a part of the journey. We'll keep asking them to join us. But, in the meantime, they cannot do anything to hinder or undermine us. If they do, then there won't be a place for them here. We will, ultimately, ask them to leave the firm.

"I know that this sounds harsh, but the firm cannot tolerate partners who dissent, feel negative about change, and want to stop others from driving forward. Our goal is to have all of our partners and people lined up behind our vision of the future.

"Each of you will need to determine whether or not you want to join us on our journey."

The room went quiet for a few seconds as Cliff's words sank in. Mark jumped quickly to his feet and pushed everyone forward again.

A picture is worth a thousand words

"The question is where and how to start things rolling. Let's go briefly back to the model we talked about at the first meeting.

Professional Service Firm Systems and Beliefs Model©

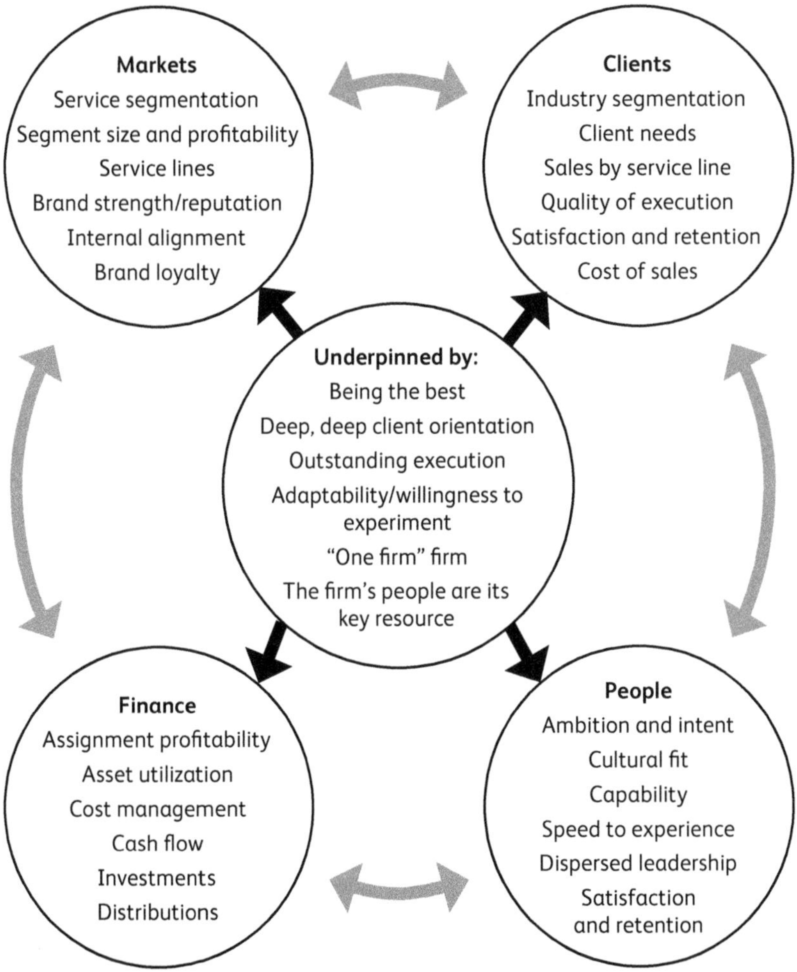

"So much of what we do is interrelated so when we ask, 'where do we start?', the answer is actually 'in lots of places'!

"The Markets Team can continue its analysis; the Clients Team can continue interviewing clients; the People Team can start developing our best-in-class learning system; the Financial Team can continue supporting the other teams and start looking at cost containment; and the Underpinning Beliefs Team can start making sure everyone knows where the firm is going, and what being the firm of choice will mean to everyone.

"But we need to be careful of overloading people – after all, we still have our normal day jobs! My suggestion is that we spend the rest of the day figuring out who will be doing what and ensure that we balance people's commitments, especially keeping in mind people's expected workload. Don't forget, you've got great support functions to help you. But they cannot decide what to do, that's your job. It's your firm! You have to take responsibility for its actions and its future.

"My other big tip is to involve the rest of the firm's people fast. In all of my experiences, immediately involving everyone across the firm in deciding how to improve the way the firm does things pays huge dividends. It's like taking the lid off the pressure cooker and watching all of this pent-up energy being unleashed. I tell you, it's amazing to watch, and so, so productive. Activities typically get done in half the time and some of the ideas can simply take your breath away. It's a huge 'win-win'.

"Okay, that's enough from me. Now it's your turn!"

Part 3

Two years later

Two years later, Kate Wellington had become the managing partner at Samson, Boyd & Johnson. She had been asked to speak to another firm about SBJ's recent journey to make SBJ the firm of choice in its chosen markets. Like Nathan's presentation to SBJ's partners two years before, Kate had a lot of interesting things to say. Let's listen to her comments.

"I wish I could tell you that there is a magic pill you can take, or a magic wand you can wave, to make everything work. You know as well as I do that is never the case. What I can tell you is that all of our partners, including me, have learned so much and we are amazed at just what can be accomplished when we work together. It hasn't been easy, nor has it been a straight line sloping upwards. We had many successes, some minor setbacks, and our fair share of failures.

"One of our core beliefs today is that it is okay to fail. We embrace, not the failures themselves, but the lessons we learn from them. This took us a while to understand and fully appreciate. Being a bunch of analytical and critical people, we were often too quick to focus on the failure, 'Why did you do that?' or, 'Why did that happen?'

"I'm more than happy to share with you what didn't go right, but I also want to make sure you get a good picture of where we were, what we did, and what did go right. Here's my agenda:

- Client and service profitability
- What has worked
- What we're struggling with
- Questions

"Let me start with the increasing client and service profitability. I expect the partners here are just like my partners. At the end of the day, they want to be rewarded for their performance and hard work. Two years ago, we set out with some financial goals. We had a three-year growth plan that focused on increasing our net income rather than just revenue growth. When we did our financial analysis, we found, like I am sure you will, that we had too many client hours that were not even contributing to our profits. I know we still have too many, but in the last two years, we have reduced the number of jobs and hours associated with our most standardized and often, as we discovered, unprofitable work, by 20 percent. That was quite an undertaking.

"Each partner had his or her list of clients that they had worked on since the dawn of time. It was like pulling teeth to persuade them to get rid of the unprofitable ones. We actually had to go through client by client with the individual partners and show them the financial impact on the firm and on their own compensation. Once they realized the consequences of keeping hold of an unprofitable client, they were much more likely to let the client go.

"But we made sure that we took care of each client. The relevant partner spoke to them about how our fees for the coming year would increase by X percent. Then the partner gave them the option of either staying with us or being referred to a smaller firm. Overall, the clients were pleased with the process and thanked us for treating them fairly.

"Partners had now freed-up some time to devote to their other, more profitable, clients or to go out into the marketplace to work on some targets or spend more time with their better referral sources. As they spent more time with their clients, we also understood more clearly our core clients and the industries they represent.

"We have moved to a matrix organization where our service lines cross our industries. We now go to market with individuals who understand the industry and have service expertise that the client wants.

"The practice segmentation matrix showed us that we shouldn't deliver every service in the same way. We still do our fair share of standardized services, as I said, but we have developed a unique team of para-professionals to deliver this work at a much lower cost. We were able to increase our realized rate per hour by over 20 percent with these clients by using lower cost, but qualified, professionals to complete the work.

"The additional dollars we earned from these changes enabled us to invest in creating a 'best-in-class' learning system for our people. One thing I am really proud of is the motivation and ambition of our people. They can see the multiple opportunities they have to develop as professionals, and they are always pushing us to make the firm go further and faster. It is very exciting to watch and witness the energy in the offices.

"Prior to starting our journey we heard a lot about trust and its importance in a professional service firm. I think we have always had an exceptional team of partners who, for the most part, trust each other. But, like anything else, you can always make it better. We have become more transparent in the way that we operate and make decisions. We set up partner teams to advise our leadership team and act as sounding boards, and this has been extremely helpful.

"We changed our compensation system from a pure formula approach that didn't reward actions that would pay off in the future to one that takes into consideration both subjective and long-term value enhancement activities. We want to make sure we reward people for doing things today that also build our capacity for the future.

"Maybe the hardest thing I had to learn to do was to make tough decisions. Three of our partners decided to leave the firm after we started on our journey. It was clear to everyone from day one that all of us had to commit to walking together as we moved our firm forward. Once it became clear that things would be different, that their compensation would change and the bar was getting higher for everyone, the three partners decided that they would be better off someplace else.

"In my discussions with each one of them, I told them I respected their decision and offered to help them find a more appropriate home. One we were able to place with a client and the other two took some of their business and went to other firms. At the end of the day, I felt our treatment of them reflected our values and upheld our reputation. And I think they did too!

"Even though Mark warned us about trying to do too much all at once, we thought we knew better. Well, guess what, Mark was right. It's not about checking things off the to-do list; it's about achieving real change in the organization. Once that became startlingly clear, we became more realistic and even a little easier on ourselves.

"We also suffered from a little change fatigue. The partners in charge of the offices and I felt that we were constantly on the move, talking day-in and day-out about change. We all got a little tired, especially as we still had our own client work to do. What made it worthwhile was every time one of our partners said, 'Okay, I get it. I know where we are going and what I need to do to help get us there. Now, get out of my office!' We all had a good laugh, and you could sense the mood in the firm swing upwards every time.

"So what are we still struggling with? After two years, we are still learning and getting better. Our goal two years ago was to become the firm of choice in our chosen markets, which meant taking the firm to the next level. Overall, we believe we have succeeded in some of our markets, but still have to work in others. But we're really pleased with what we've done so far, and we are pushing very hard to be the firm of choice in all of the markets we identified. We have, belatedly, also realized that there's no standing still and that we have to keep getting better at everything we do. In fact, we now believe that the only limit to what we can achieve is the one we set ourselves.

"Some of our partners didn't get that at first and thought that once we got to the next level, we could sit back and rest on our laurels. But they soon realized that that is just not reality. In fact, in order to stay competitive, we now know that being adaptable and open to change is the only way forward.

"I mentioned that we had set up some partner groups to advise the leadership team, and we have just created another team. Our newest team consists of our best people throughout the firm – from partners to entry level staff. Their charge is to think about changes that we will be facing in the near future. They will be helping us to predict things like what disruptive technologies or trends might impact the industries we want to focus on, what learning we should put in place to cope with them, and any changes in the workplace we need to respond to.

"When we work on a client engagement, our clients expect a definitive solution or set of actions that will yield one. Just as when we add two plus two we know we will get four. Taking a firm to the next level is not like that. First of all, the next level for your firm will be different than it was for us or will be for any of your competitors. And, although every next level will have broadly similar aspects to it, the actions each firm has to take to achieve it will likely be very different. And, when you get to that new level, as we've just found, there's always another one to strive for.

"This may seem overwhelming to some of you. I know that is how some of my partners felt. But we live in a dynamic, fluid environment. Clients, competitors, technology, and people's expectation are constantly changing. The worst thing that any firm can do is to take the attitude that it is doing every right and doesn't have to worry about getting better because it is great at what it does today.

"I also realize that no one individual has all the information needed to make the major decisions that we are faced with on a regular basis. We began our change process by using teams and found that, for us, this was an effective way to help the ongoing decision-making process. And, as I've just mentioned, we now have a number of partner groups that help guide the leadership team. The end result is that, together, we make better decisions and implement them more quickly. In today's environment that's key.

"I'm sure you are going to have questions, so let me stop here and address what's on your mind."

A final word

Well that's the end of the story.

You now know that to start your firm down the road to get to the next level and become the firm of choice, you must:

- Be clear what the next level means to your firm
- Think through what your firm needs to address in each of the five areas that drive professional service firm performance
- Agree on what needs to be done
- Prioritize your findings and then create your proposed solutions
- Start executing your plan
- Follow the successful change principles

It's quite a challenge, but remaining the firm of choice means it's something that has to be worked on constantly. None of us can ever rest on our laurels. While everything starts with deciding which services to provide, in which markets, and to which clients, at the end of the day, it's all about the skills your people have and their ability to execute. No firm can exist without its people and the key is recognizing that everyone, partners and associates, has to walk together.

Yes, the partners have to lead, but it is only when all of the firm's people march in the same direction at the same time, absolutely committed to helping the firm be the best at what it does, that any firm can become a true market leader.

A firm that is truly the firm of choice is the best at what it does and is continually challenging existing thinking and practices. It's the firm that clients and markets know delivers outstanding work, a "top of mind" firm that everyone – clients, associates, and partners – is exceptionally proud to be a part of.

If you have questions or if we can be of any service to your firm, please contact Rob at roblees2@sky.com or August at aaquila@aquilaadvisors.com or +1 952–930–1295.

Rob Lees
August Aquila

Part 4

This section contains all the exhibits and key concepts presented in this book

What successful firms do

They have a clear vision and strategies for getting there

- There is a shared understanding of what to do and shared commitment to its achievement
- They make tough choices, always focusing on continuous renewal
- The partners role model the behavior needed to deliver sustained success

They think markets as well as clients

- The partners continually scan the competitive environment
- They anticipate market changes and look for opportunities to enhance their service offering
- Having decided what to do, they invest in the resources needed to deliver

They develop a deep, deep client orientation

- Their reputation for delivering outstanding solutions precedes them
- Companies actively seek them out
- They are part of their clients' "institutional memory" – the first port of call when the client needs help

The firm's people are as important as the firm's clients

- The firm is committed to helping its people develop their expertise either inside or outside of the firm
- "It's a hard place to be hired into, a hard place to be promoted, and a hard place to stay" – but, when people move on, they do so as friends
- The firm cares about its people, going out of its way to help with both work and personal situations

They have a high performance ethos

- Everyone in the firm positively wants to be the best
- People will go the extra mile
- People actively seek new solutions which force competitors to react

They are great at execution

- They leverage ideas and expertise, regardless of their origin, to deliver client value
- People are confident enough to set stretch goals and push hard
- They focus on client solutions that are at the forefront of thinking

They embrace the "one firm" concept

- Loyalty abounds in the firm
- They downplay stars. It's the team not the individual that really matters
- There is an embedded set of principles and practices which maximize the trust and loyalty people feel for both the firm and their colleagues

They have a strong culture and shared values

- The firm has a culture of high challenge and high support
- Partners "walk together"
- People are intolerant of the "wrong" behavior

They have a highly collaborative style

- People go out of their way to help each other
- The focus is on team not individual
- People have confidence in their colleagues and proudly introduce them to their clients

They have strong partnerships

- Partners see themselves as custodians of the firm's future, creating an even better firm for the people who follow them
- Partners share and police the firm's vision, values, and strategies
- There is a premium on collegiality and discipline

They have an absolute commitment to recruiting the right people

- Top partners lead the recruitment efforts
- Cultural fit is as important as technical competence
- They downplay qualifications, focusing on the individual, not the piece of paper

They believe that developing their professionals is at the core of the firm's beliefs and activities

- Partners pass on their knowledge and expertise – continually and actively
- Coaching and mentoring are part of the foundation of the firm
- The focus is on "growing your own" rather than bringing in lateral hires

They are committed to staying at the top

- People always look for new ways of doing business
- They continually draw input from multiple and diverse sources
- Coming second isn't acceptable

Categorizing the issues

Markets

- Markets are really tough
- Competition is coming from many new competitors
- Competitors are offering new services
- Competitors are cutting prices
- We are serving each market segment the same way we always have

Clients

- Clients are spreading work among different professional service firms
- Clients are becoming more sophisticated
- Client needs and expectations are changing
- Revenue from core service lines is decreasing
- Clients are more demanding
- Clients are more price sensitive
- Clients want more value for their fees
- We are not winning enough business

People

- Best recruits are not joining the firm
- Firm is losing its up-and-coming associates
- Loss of experienced people will create succession issues
- Partners are becoming disengaged
- Partners are grumbling about issues rather than addressing them
- Associates are complaining that their friends get better training at other firms

Financial

- Revenue has been flat for three years
- Revenue from core service lines is declining
- Net profit has remained flat for three years
- Gross margins are down

- WIP days outstanding are increasing
- Clients are slower to pay
- Firm is not firing unprofitable clients

Underpinning beliefs

- Firm seems to be drifting
- No clear direction
- We accept things as they are, not what they should be
- There seems to be no urgency/things happen to us, we don't take charge
- Our compensation is not aligned with strategic issues
- We lack a clear performance management system
- Our partners don't lead

Markets questions

Markets Team questions

- Do we have a brand that is recognizable?
- Is there brand consistency?
- How loyal are our clients?
- Do we really know where our revenue comes from?
- Do we deliver services in the most efficient and profitable manner?
- Do we know how our services segment and how important each one is?
- Are we offering the right services?
- What services are our competitors offering?
- How are our services viewed compared with our competition?
- Do we know what to do to succeed in each segment?

Clients questions

Clients Team questions

- Who are our core clients?
- What do they want from us?
- How do we want them to perceive us?
- What do they buy from us and from our competitors?
- What do they value?
- What do we know about them and their business?
- Do we know which industries are growing or shrinking?
- What data about our clients do we have?
- Why have we lost clients?
- Why don't we win more proposals/opportunities?
- What's our reputation in the market?
- What do our clients think about us?
- What do our clients think about our competitors?
- Do we know who the most profitable clients are?
- What types of services are our clients no longer using?
- Which clients make us money?
- How do we want our clients to perceive us?

People questions

People Team questions

- Do we have the right people in the right roles?
- Can we attract the talent we want?
- Do we reward the right behavior and capabilities?
- Do we have effective training programs?
- Do our learning and development initiatives deliver the capabilities we need?
- Do we keep the people we want?
- Do we advance people at the right time and speed?
- Why do people leave us?
- What are we really good at?
- Are the partners and managers good coaches?
- Do our teams work as well as they should?
- Do we have the right bench strength?
- Do our people ask for help?

Financial questions

Financial Team questions

- What is our range of net realized rate per hour by client, by type of work?
- What should be our acceptable gross margin on our clients?
- How do we increase utilization by level?
- How do we improve realization?
- Can we increase partner/staff leverage?
- How do we justify higher rates?
- What is an acceptable level of net income per partner?
- How do we manage and contain cost?
- What should we be doing to make investments for the future?
- What do people spend their non-billable time doing?
- Do we have the right processes to achieve our financial goals?

Underpinning beliefs questions

Underpinning Beliefs Team questions

- Do we have a common culture? If not, what are the differences?
- Do different practices/offices have different cultures?
- Do we actually go the extra mile for our clients, or do we just talk about it?
- Are we committed to each other?
- Are we adaptable? Do we find new ways to do things?
- Do we reinvent ourselves?
- Do we care about each other?
- Does everyone play a part in the firm's future?
- Does everyone care about the firm?
- Are we creating a "one firm" firm?
- How do we get the partners to walk together?
- Does everyone know what the firm is trying to achieve?
- Is everyone committed to doing outstanding work all of the time?

Key questions

Markets Team key questions

- Do we know how the market for services is segmented and how profitable each segment is?
- What do we need to do to be successful in each of our segments?
- Do we know what services our competitors are offering and how they deliver them?

Clients Team key questions

- What do our clients buy from us, and what do they buy from our competitors?
- Which clients make us money?
- How do clients perceive us?
- What do we know about them, their business, and their industries?
- Why have we lost clients?

People Team key questions

- How do we know we have the right people in the right roles?
- How do we gain an understanding of the capabilities we need to be successful, and where our real capabilities lie?
- How can we attract the talent we want?
- Do our learning and development initiatives deliver the capabilities we need?
- Do our people consistently strive to be better? If not, why not?
- Do we reward the right behavior and competencies?

Financial Team key questions

- What is our range of net realized rate per hour by client, by type of work?
- What should be our acceptable gross margin on our clients?
- What should we be doing to make investments in our future?

Underpinning Beliefs Team key questions

- How do we get the partners to walk together?
- How do we make sure that everyone knows what the firm is trying to achieve?
- How adaptable are we? Do we find new ways to do things?
- Do we actually go the extra mile for our clients, or do we just talk about it?
- Do we have a common culture? If not, what are the differences?

Professional Service Firm Systems and Beliefs Model©

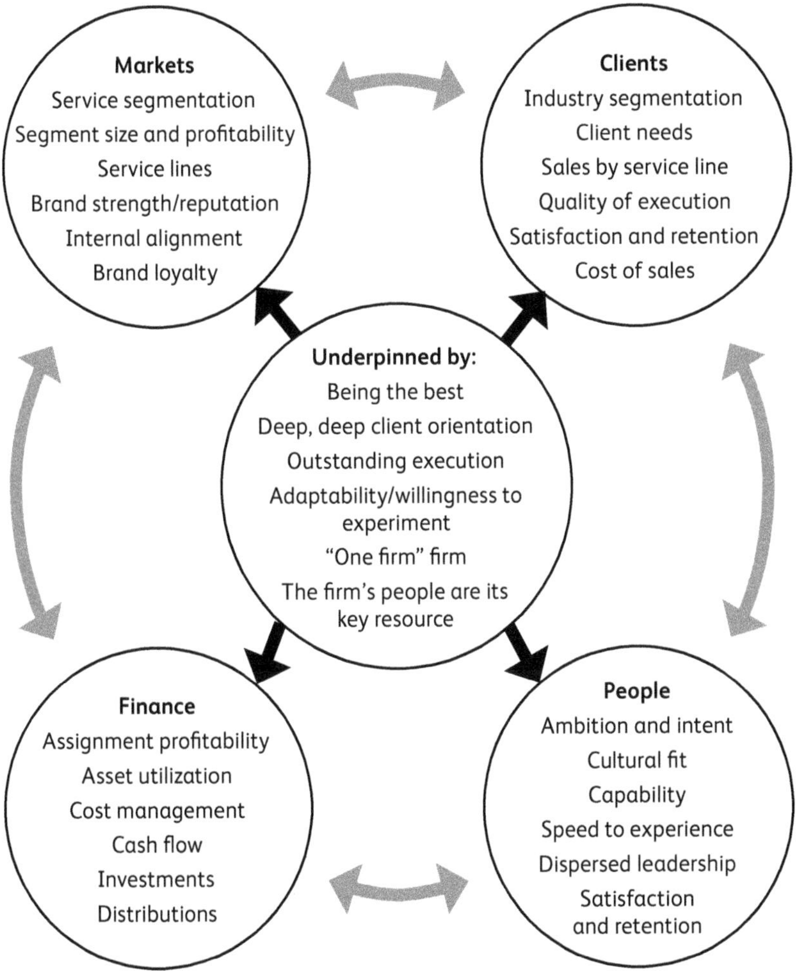

Professional Service Firm Systems and Beliefs Model in Action©

Practice Segmentation in Professional Services

Standardized	Customized	Expertise-Driven	Rocket Science
Client Problem: Efficient solutions to common problems	**Client Problem:** A tailored, but still relatively low cost, solution to a common problem; guidance through the pre- and post-purchasing process	**Client Problem:** A major complex and ill-defined issue that the client has little or no experience of	**Client Problem:** A major "bet your company" issue that the client has no similar experience of
Key Skill: Efficient, low cost delivery of established methodologies, models, and processes	**Key Skill:** Providing user-friendly advice which generates confidence in the selection process and thereafter	**Key Skill:** Real-time diagnosis and judgment	**Key Skill:** Providing innovative and novel solutions
Critical Success Factors: Established methodologies, models, and processes; efficient and low cost delivery systems	**Critical Success Factors:** Established methodologies, models, and processes; efficient, low cost delivery systems; inter-personal/relationship skills; managing the "sales" costs	**Critical Success Factors:** Experience of similar problems; in-depth technical and/or functional knowledge; exceptional relationship skills	**Critical Success Factors:** Highest level diagnostic skills; creativity; state of the art knowledge; pioneering concepts
Profit Drivers: High volume, high leverage	**Profit Drivers:** Above average fees; good leverage	**Profit Drivers:** High fees; low leverage	**Profit Drivers:** Premium fees; very low leverage; may also refer work to others
Selling Proposition: "Better, faster, cheaper"	**Selling Proposition:** "Use us, we'll tailor the solution to you and your needs, and provide you with ongoing support"	**Selling Proposition:** "Trust us, we've seen similar problems before and we'll help you over your problems"	**Selling Proposition:** "Smartest brains around"

Adapted from the original matrix, ©Rob Lees and Jack Gabarro, which is included in When Professionals Have to Lead, *Harvard Business School Press, 2007*

Markets Team proposals

- Prepare an in-depth analysis of our services segments
- Analyze how we go to market
- Determine what success looks like in each segment and compare that to how we go to market
- In conjunction with the Clients Team, analyze each segment to find out which industries and clients our firm serves, and to what scale
- Have the firm's marketing department conduct a competitor analysis

Clients Team proposals

- Prepare an in-depth market analysis of our clients and their industries
- Conduct interviews with our top 20–40 clients to determine what work we are not getting
- Work with the Financial Team to analyze the gross margins we get on our top clients
- Work with Markets Team to develop a questionnaire to understand client perception of the firm and satisfaction
- Provide industry research and training for partners and managers to help them understand our clients' businesses
- Interview lost clients to determine why they left us

What is a market?

A market is a group of potential clients with a common need where we have the services/products that can satisfy the need.

People Team proposals

- Analyze our non-technical and technical capabilities and compare them to market needs both now and in the future. Fill in any gaps in current and required capabilities
- Determine what standards are required to be the firm of choice and ensure that leaders drive performance to those standards
- Make sure that there is clarity about what people have to do. Help them understand what they need to do better
- Communicate the "new" firm to potential new entrants and ensure we recruit the people we want
- Develop a "world class" learning system

The best practice learning model

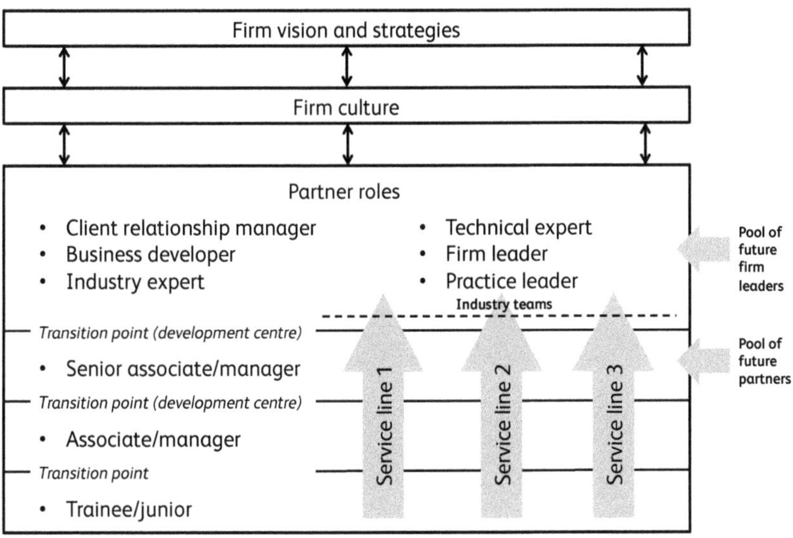

Financial Team proposals

- Analyze the firm's net realized rate per hour by client segment and by service segment
- Analyze the top ten clients by partner to determine average gross margins
- Determine what percentage of our profits should be allocated for investment projects that will build capacity for us in the future

Four streams of content

- Technical – including project management/assignment efficiency
- Winning business – individually and in teams
- Analyzing businesses – understanding client strategies and positioning the firm's services
- Leading and managing teams – at assignment, practice, and firm level

Underpinning Beliefs Team proposals

- Create a "one firm" firm by reinforcing the partners' understanding of what it means to be a partner in our firm. And then help our partners create it!
- Communicate the firm's plan and initiatives to everyone in the firm using as many different types of media as possible. And keep doing it!
- Support the partners in driving a culture of innovation and change
- Look for great client service examples within the firm and publicize and promote them as best practices
- Identify, define, and provide examples of our shared values in action. Evaluate our people on how well they live the values and, when it's needed, help them live the values more consistently

From...	To
• Undermining colleagues and the firm's initiatives	• Supporting firm initiatives by participating
• Subverting ideas discussed at partner meetings	• Presenting evidence based on alternatives
• Treating staff poorly	• Treating all staff with respect
• Staying silent, not voicing objections when decisions are made	• Communicating concerns openly and providing alternative solutions
• Finding fault in everyone and every idea	• Focusing on team members' strengths and helping them develop

"Ideally, I'd love to walk you through the initiatives in the same topic-based way, but change doesn't happen in a straight line. The reality is that what you do in one area nearly always impacts another, so change has to be seen as holistic – a series of interrelated initiatives, which, over time, lead to changes in the way the firm does things and, ultimately, to an improvement in economic performance."

"And then our big break happened. It was an absolutely unplanned result. But we found out that that's the way some things happen when you undertake a change initiative. You embrace it and use it and move on at speed!"

Selected other works by the authors

Aquila, A.J. and Lees, R.J. *How to Engage Partners in the Firm's Future*, Bay Street Group, 2013.

Aquila, A.J. and Rice, C. *Compensation as a Strategic Asset,* AICPA, 2017.

Aquila, A.J. and Rice, C. *Performance Is Everything*, AICPA, 2012.

Aquila, A.J. and Marcus, B. *Client at the Core*, John Wiley and Sons, 2004.

DeLong, T.J., Gabarro, J.J., and Lees, R.J. *When Professionals Have to Lead: A New Model for High Performance*, Harvard Business School Press, 2007.

DeLong, T.J., Gabarro, J.J., and Lees, R.J. "Why mentoring matters in a hypercompetitive world", *Harvard Business Review*, January 2008.

Lees, R.J., Aquila, A.J. and Klyhn, D. *What Successful Managing Partners Do*, Bay Street Group, 2013.

Lees, R.J., Aquila, A.J. and Klyhn, D. "Speed to experience: Winning the game", *Of Counsel*, October 2012 and *Managing Partner*, May 2013.

Lees, R.J., Aquila, A.J. and Klyhn, D. "One size does not fit all: Segmenting services drives professional services marketing and sales", *Of Counsel* and *Managing Partner*, both March 2014.

Lees, R.J. and Aquila, A. J. "Superior dimensions", *Of Counsel*, May 2015.

Lees, R.J. and Mister, M.L. "What HR should really do", *Of Counsel*, December 2016.

Lees R.J. and Mister, M.L. "Making centralization and agility a reality", *Of Counsel*, July 2014.

www.ingramcontent.com/pod-product-compliance
Ingram Content Group UK Ltd.
Pitfield, Milton Keynes, MK11 3LW, UK
UKHW021846150926
8657IPUK00005B/96

9 781783 582723